Emmanue.

I stand in the presence of God. Luke 1:19

Bill Pruitt

ISBN: 9798387287589

Cover design by: Art Painter

Library of Congress Control Number: 2018675309

Printed in the United States of America

Acknowledgments

This book is dedicated to:

My sweet Barbie, wife, and love of my life. Thanks for enduring this journey with me and all that we have yet to come. I have come to love you with an enduring love for all eternity. I know without you my life would have lacked the happiness that made me who I am.

Many thanks to my parents, Don and Louise who endured the burden of discipleship to grow me in my walk with Jesus. I would like to thank my friends and family who gave me so much material to write about. Had it not been for you, my life would have lacked the wonderment I have cherished knowing you. I especially want to thank my daughter Mandy and her husband Jon along with their three children Tristen, Brooklyn, and Oakley. I also want to send my great appreciation to my son Nick and his wife Adrelly along with their three sons Harvey, Rex, and Flint. Best family ever with so many memories that I cherish.

I guess this also belongs in acknowledgements. I want to thank all those disciples who served alongside of me in the various churches and ministries to which I belonged. If it had not been for our fellowship together, I could not have experienced God in such a way to tell such amazing stories about His presence with me. It was your prayers and our struggles together that helped me find our Savior just when I needed Him most.

Finally, I want to recognize two young boys that inspired me to keep writing. To that great Big Foot hunter and nephew, Duke Pruitt, I made sure your name had a place in this book. I also want to thank Silas Jenson who seemed to enjoy my first book so much, I just felt the need to keep writing. Thanks for being a fan.

Contents

Preface

My wife said I should write another book. I guess there were still stories to be told. I can say this book will be very different than the last book, Emanuel's Laughter, in that it is less about funny stories and more about the intense experiences I have had with God. The book will still have short stories and you will still enjoy the experience of those short and meaningful chapters. I might even recommend this as a devotional reading as each chapter highlights God's teaching in my life. This book will grab your heart as you hear from my heart as I try to express the times in my life when I was so much in the presence of God, I could not only feel Him near, but I could see Him at work around me. At times I felt I could just reach out and hold onto Him.

These stories need to be told. Not because I want to impress anyone with the spirituality of my own life. I am far from anything worthy of such stories. I simply was blessed to bear witness and be a vessel of God's plans and message at these intervals of my life.

2 Corinthians 10:17 says what I feel more than anything else I can think of at this time. **But, "Let the one who boasts, boast in the Lord."** I am compelled to share these stories so you can know from yet another believer that God is near and all powerful and all compassionate and all loving. This life is difficult most of the time. We toil and we struggle through life to sustain the necessities of living. We are also blessed and happy to have loving friends and families to enrich our journey. But living is so much richer when we encounter God in a very personal way. It is those very experiences that allow me to awake each day knowing this is a day the Lord has

made for me. I am to live it, enjoy it and trust God's provision for that day. And, when my journey in this world is over and I prepare to meet my Savior, I will embrace that moment with all the experiences I have lived which taught me how to fall in love with my Lord and my God.

So, get ready to hear my boastful stories when I experienced the presence of God. It would be my prayer these stories are a reminder to you to always look for God. He is ever present in your life. He will do the absolute unexpected and afterwards there is nothing left for you to do but take joy in the experience of His presence.

You don't have to be special in this world to experience the presence of God, you just have to be special to God.

Chapter One: A Misunderstood Calling

Being confident of this, that he who began a good work in you will carry it on to completion until the day of Christ Jesus. Philippians 1:6

What is a "Calling"? When I was a young boy, I would hear about people talking about how they had been called by God. They would usually be called to be either a Pastor or a Missionary. I never really heard anyone get up in the pulpit and talk about any other kind of calling. It could leave a boy confused about God's calling to service and ministry.

You might recall if you read my first book, my dad was a Pastor. He was a good one as well. He Loved God and what was even more amazing was he loved God's people. I always thought that was the hardest part of the job because God's people were not always lovable. Yet I watched my father serve year after year. His service to God was serving God's people. His phone would ring day and night with people wanting to talk to him about their problems and predicaments. These calls would even come on Holidays. Oh yeah, even Christmas was no match for God's people and their need to be loved. Some of the most interesting living happened on the holidays. People would get themselves into all kinds of messes and then call the preacher man hoping he could help them find their way back to civility. It was a thankless but very rewarding occupation for my father. Despite the sacrifices he had to make for the ministry, there are many memories of good friendships that carried our family along.

On a rare occasion someone in the Church would respond to the call of God and tell the Church they had also been called to be a Pastor. On even more rare occasions there would be someone who would say they had been called to be a missionary. Now that was quite the event because most of the missionaries, I ever heard about had to go to some dangerous country where they were out to either imprison, kill, and eat missionaries. That did not sound like any way to live that I could get my head into. But clearly these servants followed their calling in the ministry, and they followed where God chose them to serve.

I say all this to give some perspective into the mind of a twelve-year-old boy who felt the calling. I knew deep within my heart God wanted more from me than just to warm a chair on Sunday worship. He had something in mind for me and I had to take ownership of that calling and commit my life to it. The only question I had in my mind was whether to be a missionary or a pastor. I wasn't really clear on that part of the calling. All I could remember was the calling from God to set my life apart in service to him. So, since it was unclear, I assumed the choice was up to me. As I was not fond of the idea of being a missionary, then I had to be a pastor. So, one Sunday, I told the church I was surrendering to be a pastor. That's actually how people said it back in the day. It was a surrendering kind of thing. If you could have felt the immense calling of God, you would understand there was nothing left to do but surrender. While I surrendered, I was far from defeated. I had so much to learn and so much to experience about this calling. It's a good thing I was only twelve at the time. If I had been more mature, I don't think I could have taken any pleasure in my calling. Being a minister was a difficult path in life. Good thing I had the heart of a child and just wanted to follow Jesus.

Pretty soon the church wanted to get me up in a pulpit to preach at them. So, I started preparing to deliver my first sermon. I studied for weeks and prepared notes just as I had seen my dad do in his own preparations. I didn't ask for much help, but my dad did suggest I share what God had put on my heart.

The announcement was made. There would be a guest speaker at the church on a certain Sunday and that young Billy would be preaching for us that day. As the time approached, I took my bible in my hand and walked up to the pulpit. I looked at the congregation and shared my heart. The sermon topic was simple as it was titled, "The Choice Is Yours". In the next five to seven minutes, I began to explain in a very dictatorial and logical sequence of points outlining the choices people in that congregation had. They could either choose God and spend an eternity with him or they could be brainless and not choose God and spend their eternity in Hell. It made perfect sense to me. The congregation looked a bit stunned, but the truth was the truth. I think they were stunned because they had never seen a boy my age lay out the gospel choice so bluntly. There was no place in that message for grace or forgiveness. It was only do or die.

Afterward, most everyone came to my support by encouraging me by saying what a great job I did and how proud they were of my efforts. I just didn't quite understand why the alter call didn't have every lost soul at the alter praying to receive God as their Savior. In fact, I was quite concerned with the lack of results and considered my entire effort a failure. Had I known then what I know now, I would have understood this was the first clue that I had a calling from God, but I got it all wrong.

As I grew older, I became somewhat of a curiosity for churches who would ask me to come to their church and fill in for their pastor who was out for vacation or some other reason. I would travel around West Tennessee and later Western Washington doing just that. At one point, I had a church ask me to serve as a youth pastor. That's when I began to realize that loving God's people was not simple. Later I took a position at a church as their Worship and Youth minister. By this time, I was married. we had even had our first child. The demands of working full time and serving in the church as a pastor was testing my limits as a new husband and father. But as this was the calling, I had to persist.

I had lost all patience with the Youth group. These young people were some of the most unreliable people in God's family. They get all excited about something and then they don't even bother to show up. Worship planning was equally challenging to me. I loved to worship and sing praise to God. But having to plan these services and coordinate with others to deliver that experience was causing me great frustration. I got to the point that I fired the volunteer choir for their lack of commitment to the program. I then proceeded to work with just the instrumentalist to deliver the worship time and much of that time was done with my own guitar. The freedom of just doing it myself always got the job done but clearly, I had missed the big picture.

As all this became clear to me, I turned to God and asked Him to clarify my calling. I knew without any doubt there was a calling, but I was not doing very well at this pastor thing, and I clearly was not good at leading volunteers. What had become of my life to be at this place. This is not what I expected. I resigned my position at the church and started a process of soul searching for the clarity I needed which would propel me into the rest of my ministry.

Not bad for a twelve-year-old boy. While I answered the calling, I got the wrong number. But it wasn't too late to hit redial and figure out my way forward. I don't want to share too much yet but as you read the following chapters, you can start to see how my calling was absolutely genuine. But it was not vocational. In fact, it was incredibly ordinary and was the calling God puts to every believer. God worked on my rough edges some and started shaping me into the servant He needed.

When I stopped serving traditions and religious expectations within the church and started looking forward to what God really wanted from the church and particularly from myself, my life opened into a world of possibility that could only be experienced with God and by loving his people. Joy has been restored in my heart and my strength has been renewed in my service to God. By following the calling, I am now able to profess without hesitation, God chooses all his people to serve with their whole heart. When you choose to surrender to God's calling to follow Jesus, you will experience the unimaginable. Do not be overly surprised that the Creator of Heaven and Earth is right in the midst of every challenge you face and every decision you make. Most of all He is there in the midst of the joy we experience. Life is an ordeal, and this ordeal will not be over until God calls his family home. In the meantime, we can experience God in this life as he stands alongside us on the journey to our heavenly home.

Chapter Two: Go West Young Man

Behold, I will put a fleece of wool on the threshing floor. If there is dew on the fleece only, and it is dry on all the ground, then I will know that You will deliver Israel through me, as You have spoken." And it was so. When he arose early the next morning and squeezed the fleece, he drained the dew from the fleece, a bowl full of water. Judges 6:37-38

By the time I had reached the age of seventeen, I was about to strike out into the world and find my own way. As a senior in high school, my parents decided (more my dad than my mom) to move to Kent, Washington, and pastor a startup church which was to be called Covington Baptist Church. I don't think we could have moved much further away from West Tennessee and still be in the United States. The new church had a very small congregation. In fact, when our family of five joined the congregation, the church just more than doubled. The church was a church plant from another church in Kent who would provide some financial support to the church until they could stand on their own. The church would meet at a Grange building where we would have to set up folding chairs each week for services and then break everything down and put it back in the small trailer my dad had prepared for this very purpose.

My life was going pretty well at that point. I lived just a couple hours away from my Granny who outside of my parents was the most important person in my life. I always enjoyed driving up to Paris Tennessee to spend time with her. The thought of leaving her and my Granddaddy was not going to be easy. I had friends but none of them compared with the love for my grandparents. I was also doing very well in high school. My grades were strong, and I had already secured a strong SAT score which was setting me up for college. I had discussions underway with the University of Tennessee for a scholarship and my dad's university also offered a scholarship program to their pastor's children. Since I was called to the ministry, I had serious thoughts about attending Union University in nearby Jackson Tennessee. I could likely live at home and commute to school. Now that we were leaving, I had to make choices about my own life. In fact, my parents encouraged me to consider what I needed to do as I was old enough to live with my Granny and finish high school, which would have allowed me to continue my education at one of these universities.

If this was not the biggest conundrum of my life already, my Granny sure did not make it any easier. My initial thought was to just stay with Granny and make a life for myself somehow. But then we took a trip to Kent Washington. I met the church and I saw the opportunity to serve God. I now had a difficult choice to make, and my heart was pulling in all directions.

After returning from the initial trip to Kent, my parents took us camping one last time as a family out to Kentucky Lake where we had camped and fished many times before. It was a beautiful day there. My dad had upgraded from tent camping to a Winnebago recreational vehicle. It wasn't new but it was his. Dad always felt he needed such a vehicle as we always lived in homes provided by the local church where he pastored. If he was without a church, we would be otherwise homeless without our RV. Made sense to our family even though most of the church members thought this was way to frivolous for a poor pastor. On this particular trip, we were indeed about to be homeless as my father had resigned his church position and we had just a few weeks to move out of the parsonage provided by the church. There was no turning back now. Our family was going to have to transition no matter how difficult this was about to become.

Resting in a lounge chair under a big pine tree at the campsite, I began to pray. My prayer was pretty simple, "God, what do you want me to do? Should I stay in Tennessee, or should I also respond to the calling to serve this small church in Washington?" I spent hours laying under that tree looking up through its strong branches into the heavens hoping for direction from God. The more I prayed the more the Sprit within me was making this decision clear to me. I began to understand all the ramifications of either choice. But to that point I had not clearly understood how to proceed. Then a squirrel appeared in the tree way up at the top and started to come closer to me as he creep slowly down the massive tree trunk and stopped about six feet above my head. That old red squirrel was just staring at me. I thought to myself, this is odd. Why would a wild squirrel come so close to me. I had hunted these creatures all my life and had never known one of them to be quite so eager to approach a person. That's when it hit me.

The Holy Spirit started to remind me of Gideon. Specifically, I was thinking about how Gideon asked for a sign from God to confirm His calling to lead God's people against the Midianites. I could hear God speak to me. He assured me it would be alright to ask for a sign as that is why the squirrel was there. So, I put the question to God. I said, "God, if you want me to go to Washington then have that squirrel come down closer to me. If not, then have that squirrel run back up that tree as fast as he can, and I will know my life is to be in Tennessee." See, I had already made this more difficult to go to Washington as the squirrel had to come closer to me which was not a natural behavior for a red squirrel. Especially since I had decided to move my chair a bit closer to the tree and put my head right up against that tree. The natural behavior for a squirrel would have been to run aways as soon as he saw me move. But do you know that old squirrel sat there and watched me? I could have stood up and grabbed him as he was already so close to me. After I repositioned myself against that tree and before I really got settled and comfortable, that squirrel came right down that tree towards my head. I would say he was about six inches away from me when I realized there was no escaping the clarity of what had just happened. God made it ever so clear to me my life and my ministry were going to be in Washington. It was important to surrender to that decision quickly, because if I waited any longer, I am pretty certain God would have sent that squirrel down on my head, and I would had needed to go to a doctor for rabies shots. I did not want to get into it with a God purposed squirrel.

Afterward, I felt God's presence fill me so full my soul burst open with worship. Tears of joy and surrender poured down my face as I was about to experience what God had next for me. I knew there were some very hard things to experience before we left, one of which was helping my Granny understand I had also been called to serve in Washington. Granny had a powerful love for me, and this was not going to be easy. In fact, I recall the morning we pulled out of her driveway with our caravan of vehicles to head west, she was screaming for my dad to leave and do what he had to do but not to take her babies away from her. As a grandparent now, I feel her pain and her loneliness watching her love drive away. It was all I could do to stay in the truck with my dad as we pulled away. But God was there reminding me about that squirrel. I sure didn't need to have another encounter with a

God possessed squirrel no matter how difficult this was going to be. And believe me I had no idea how challenging and rewarding my life was about to become.

Chapter Three: From God's Hands to My Belief

Not that I speak in respect of want: for I have learned, in whatsoever state I am, therewith to be content. Philippians 4:11

The drive west had started and in accordance with my father's preferred driving style, we only stopped to refill with gas until we had reached our destination. That's right, we would drive day and night eating Slap-Wiches all the way. For all you non-southerners reading this story, a Slap-Wich is a sandwich made with two pieces of white bread with bologna and mustard inside. A person could prepare a slap-wich for a driver upon request from the cooler stored on the floorboard next to the driver.

My dad and I drove a reconditioned refrigerator truck packed to the max towing my Toyota Corolla. The little car was over packed such that a driver would have had to unload a good portion of the contents just to enter the vehicle. My mom, brother and sister were driving a brand-new Dodge Maxi-van with only one seat for the driver. The rest of the van was packed with our belongings and my brother and sister sat on dining room chairs while pulling a ragged old trailer packed well over its load limit. The old truck would barely keep up freeway speeds. So, the idea was to have my dad lead out and my mom would follow him. I would take turns providing relief shifts of driving for my dad and then my mom. My dad only had one rule about the trip besides preparing a Slap-Wich on his orders and that was never to pull off without passing the truck first and directing our small caravan to the next exit. This way we would all stay together for the long trip to Washington.

We had just made it to Kansas City and were heading west out of town on the freeway. All was going well as we began to drive into the cornfields. My dad checked his rearview mirror and noticed the van was not following us. He slowed the old truck to give my mom time to catch up. Then he pulled off to the shoulder to wait for my mom to catch up. After several minutes, we both concluded my mom must have had vehicle troubles and needed assistance. Since we didn't have cell phones back in the day, we drove to the next exit, returned to the eastbound freeway to find my mom. We had not traveled very far until we saw our blue Dodge maxivan flying down the freeway at speeds in excess of 80 mph with the trailer in tow. My dad turned and looked at me in amazement. I remember him saying, "Son, say goodbye to your mother. We may never see her again until we get to Seattle."

We quickly returned to the westbound freeway traveling at maximum speed near 60 mph. We had rationalized that my mom might give chase to us for a short while before realizing she had overtaken us and then pull off the freeway and wait for us. Given we had been separated for about ten minutes, and the van was traveling in excess of 80 mph, her ability to catch that old truck was well within a ten minute chase. We drove for hours looking at each exit hoping to find them waiting for us. We drove the entire day and just before we entered Colorado, we saw the blue Dodge maxivan on the shoulder of the freeway. Mom had traveled at a high speed for about 400 miles hoping to overtake the truck. She waited on the side of the road for just over two hours while we caught up with her. While my mom was pretty good with numbers, in a panic she clearly put all reason aside and pressed onward. She was about to call my granny and ask for assistance, which would have been more trouble for the family. Fortunately, that old truck got there just before she was about to head back to Tennessee.

This was the beginning of a great adventure which would try our faith and commitment as a family. When mom and dad reconnected, they were thrilled for a moment until my dad started trying to rationalize what my mom had done and get her to reason about the speed of the truck. My mom wasn't having it. Seems she only pulled over for a moment to assist my little sister before returning to the road. In her mind this was very acceptable and didn't require adherence to any rules laid out by my father. Not sure these two ever agreed on the best practice but this was just the first of many family trials to come.

After we arrived in Washington, my dad found a rental house we couldn't afford. It wouldn't have mattered what house he found, we really couldn't afford a house but had to have one anyway. The home was located in a subdivision called Timberlane. Timberlane was in the Covington area where our church was to be located. The early days of establishing the new church ministry were spiritually rewarding but tested our faith beyond measure. It took a while to get enough financial support to make the income close enough to the bills so that we could have any hope of paying them. Food became the variable expense in the family finances. I can remember mornings when our family would come together and pray because the bills were due. We were short hundreds of dollars needed to cover them. On one such day this happened, and my mom was anxious as we didn't have anything much in the house to eat. The refrigerator was near empty, and the pantry just had a couple of cans of stuff that wouldn't compliment an actual meal.

My dad went to the mailbox that afternoon and opened four envelopes. Each containing a check from people we knew wanting to assist our family with this ministry. Just in time there was enough money to cover the bills and buy a bag of tortilla chips from the store. My resourceful mom had figured out a way to cobble together a meal of Nachos. First time our family ever had Nachos, and wouldn't you know we had just enough to get us through that dinner. The next day the church paid my dad and we got to go grocery shopping. It's a great feeling to see food in the house. My mom was always at ease when she had the ability to feed her family.

God always knew exactly where our family was and what we needed. This happened so many times during the first years starting the ministry at Covington Baptist Church that we never doubted God was watching and would provide a way forward. It would come in several ways and was always a blessing. But that one day when the checks came to the mailbox, God put my own heart at ease and assured me the chaos around me was just chaos. The promises He had made to provide for my needs were worth more than any bank account or pantry of food.

Not only did God bless our family but also the work in the church was starting to become very rewarding. The small congregation which started with nine on our first day meeting in a Grange Hall just outside Kent Washington was now reaching souls who were seeking a Savior. My job was to lead the youth group and to lead the music for worship. I also had to set up and tear down the grange hall each week for services. We stayed busy about the Lord's work, and God blessed our family in ways to this day I will always remember as my anchor in faith. I still reflect on the decision to move west as the sacrifice at the time seemed monumental. But then to experience God's care and faithfulness gave me such a sense of purpose and value in God's Kingdom. While the struggles continued so did the blessings from heaven.

To this day I love Nachos and still think about how God continues to provide for me.

Chapter Four: Alder to Alter

Look at the birds of the air; they do not sow or reap or store away in barns, and yet your heavenly Father feeds them. Are you not much more valuable than they? 27 Can any one of you by worrying add a single hour to your life? "And why do you worry about clothes? See how the flowers of the field grow. They do not labor or spin. Yet I tell you that not even Solomon in all his splendor was dressed like one of these. If that is how God clothes the grass of the field, which is here today and tomorrow is thrown into the fire, will he not much more clothe you—you of little faith? Mathew 6:26-30

As the ministry at the church continued, I graduated from high school and started night school for college. I started with a satellite program study from the University of Washington offered by a community college near my home. I majored in Business Administration and minored in Accounting. I also got my first full-time job at a bank operations center. I was tasked with microfilming checks before they were posted to bank accounts and then spent the afternoons completing copy request for customers of checks needed for their records and/or subpoenas. Every morning I would get up from my bed at my parent's home, head for work and then go to school that evening. I would usually get back home in time to go to bed and start the routine over again. This was my routine except for weekends where I worked with the church doing various ministry assignments and cutting down trees on the church property.

That's right. This small congregation was able to purchase ten acres of land right on the main road running through Covington.

It was covered in timber and brush. We had a future church home. The small congregation went right to work trying to make our way from the Grange Hall to this new location. The thought of not having to set up chairs every Sunday morning was a driving force in my determination to help get us moved. Not sure if you have ever tried to experience worship after a full workout usually with light perspiration. It's not exactly the way I used to get ready for Sunday worship. I think the congregation wanted me to lead the music because that kept me away from everyone else as my Speed Stick was running out of speed.

While the church had much to do to find a way to pay for a new church building, we did need to start clearing land. My dad decided to purchase a mobile home for the family which he would locate on the church property well behind the location for the new church building. It was a great day when we moved into the new home. It also gave us access to the work at hand. Cutting trees and managing brush burn piles became my weekend activity. We cut enough alder and maple to help pay for the land and get us on our way to starting construction on the church building.

A man affiliated with the church loaned us a small dozer just tough enough to pull a tree log and push a stump to the burn pile. Clearing trees was also important to keep them from falling on our new home as well as keeping the wood stove heated for winter temperatures. I am not even sure why the college required me to take a physical education class. I was more buff chopping wood than I had ever been during high school sporting activities.

One day I was falling an alder tree near our house as my dad was concerned the windstorms would blow it over on the house. I got pretty good at dropping trees. However, this particular tree was worrisome. I had been thinking about how to fall that tree. I decided to get the small dozer which had a winch and attach it to the tree to give me control over the drop. I cut through the tree taking a perfect wedge out of the tree base making sure it would fall in the direction I desired. Using the dozer, I even secured the winch line up higher on the tree to further insure it fell where I wanted it to drop. I then used wedge blocks on the reverse side to further influence the drop of the tree away from the house. Once I had everything just right, I returned to the dozer and started to take up the winch line and that big alder tree started to fall exactly where I wanted it to fall. The early morning crash of the tree was just outside my parent's bedroom window startled them, and my dad came running out of the house to find the tree had fallen on top of the dozer with me inside the cage. Now that I think about it, it might not had been the crash of the tree but rather my screaming for help that caused him to come running. Fortunately, this dozer had a safety cage for the operator. I couldn't get out of the cage as I was submersed in alder tree branches.

My dad grabbed the chainsaw and started efforts to cut me out of the dozer. I sustained no damage, but I did break a hydraulic line on the dozer which I could now repair as I had a job with money coming in. Seems most of my discretionary income was spent on fixing things I would damage in those days. There wasn't much discretionary income after I paid for schooling and gas. But since I was useful around home chopping wood on the weekends, my dad tolerated me. Living at home during those years was a blessing as I would not have been able to graduate debt free if I had also been paying housing cost. But God provided even for my education which was going to be just what I needed to establish a career in the financial technology industry.

Eventually I was able to purchase a new car as my blossoming career brought in a bit more discretionary income. I was moving up big time from my 69 Toyota Corolla to a power blue 1980 Nissan 210. It got great gas mileage, but it wasn't much for power or to demonstrate one's emerging masculinity.

I tell all this to make one point incredibly clear. I was a busy young man. I had answered a calling to serve in a new church start up, was getting my education as I was certain this would be necessary supporting the move into full time pastoral ministries, and I was also holding a full-time job. My mom used to tell me she knew I was still alive because the pile of dirty clothes kept growing. That's about all she saw of me until we got to church again on Sunday. I was on a fast track to finish a three year pre-professional degree in two years by taking full semester loads and attending summer classes. By early 1982 I was tired, lonely, and almost finished with my initial degree. I really wasn't sure what was coming next, but I was committed to the work to get there. People would ask me about dating and while I would do a little bit of that, there was really no time to consider a serious relationship in my life. Just when I thought I was doing exactly what I was supposed to do, God showed up and blessed me in a very unexpected way.

In my other book, I shared the story of how I met my wife, Barb. Part of the resistance to meeting Barb was my life plan. But then again, my plan was not lining up with God's plan anymore. God put Barb in my life and turned everything upside down. I had just one more class to complete at college to get my degree. But when I fell in love, I decided to come back to that later. I remember the first date with Barb. We went to a Mexican restaurant called Azteca. Seems she liked Mexican food. Afterwards we were going to see a movie. I believe it was Raiders of the Lost Ark. That was a big plan for a first date. I picked Barb up and the two of us started to discover each other.

Sometimes when we follow God we get so busy in the mission we forget to live the life God wants to have us experience. I truly believe it gives God pleasure to see His plans for us bring joy and happiness in this troubled world. This all started to make sense to me as this first date proceeded. I'll never forget what we ordered for dinner that night. I had a hearty appetite, so I ordered a thing called a Chalupa. It was basically the biggest taco I had ever seen. But Barb did something that surprised me. She ordered Nachos. Wouldn't you know it, but this sweet gal loved Nachos and to this day it is one of her favorite meals. Coincidence? I think not.

Clearly God blessed my conviction and commitment despite my flailing efforts to serve Him. Believe me when I say I was not deserving of the blessings that were coming my way. Everyone says hindsight is 20/20. What a joy it is to know that when you ask God for a sign to help your faith and then commit to Him when He says, "Follow Me", He is faithful in every way and the blessings from Heaven are more than I can behold.

Not to boast of my faithfulness to God but rather His faithfulness to me has made all the difference. I just take little steps of faith and before you know it I have a lifetime of experiences demonstrating God's faithfulness. I treasure each and every experience as it helps me face the next thing. God knew before I could even recognize my own need what I needed to be fulfilled in this life. He knew all this before he sent that squirrel down the tree to me. Had I not moved to Seattle, I would have never met Barbie. I would not have spent a career in Financial Technology and had great fulfillment doing so. I would not have experienced the blessings of having my two wonderful children, their spouses and all those amazing grandchildren.

Truly there is no better thing anyone can do in this life but to seek God and trust his plans to provide for all your needs. While this got me to the alter in Holy Matrimony, this was still just the beginning of many more experiences where I knew the presence of God and could see his provision for me.

Chapter Five: Give Tithe or Rob God

Will a man rob God? Yet you have robbed me. But you say, Where have we robbed God? In tithes and offerings. You are cursed with a curse: for you have robbed me, even this whole nation. Bring all the tithes into the storehouse, that there may be meat in my house, and prove me now, says the Lord of hosts, if I will not open unto you the windows of heaven, and pour you out a blessing, that there shall not be room enough to receive it. Malachi 3:8-10

One would think as good as God had already been to me in my life, I would not struggle with obedience to His teachings. But like every newlywed, we never seemed to have enough money to do anything but barely exist. One would think I would get used to that way of living but I struggled with the struggle. As I first entered into marriage, I had a big decision to make. Before I married Barb, I had committed $35 a month to the church building program. There was a financial commitment program our small church went through before we started building our church building to demonstrate the congregation had enough means to meet a loan payment for the construction. Thirty five dollars back in the day is more like three hundred dollars today. Before we got married Barb and I discussed this commitment and decided we should be faithful to my pledge and finish this three-year commitment of which we had about another year to go.

The first year of marriage is a financial challenge. There are so many things needed to just get your household going. I still don't know how we made it in those days. But somehow Barb would pick up a few extra dollars from child care and my work was advancing and providing more income to pay the bills. I remember the day we made the last payment to the building fund. I felt we had fulfilled our obligation and were free now to enjoy a bit of discretionary income. My attitude was about to bring me down. Barb and I had left the church in Covington to start serving as an Associate Pastor in another church where I lead the worship and youth ministries. We both had a love in our hearts for the church at Covington, but we also felt it was time for us to start engaging in the work to fulfill my commitment to serve God as a pastor.

With school set aside, I now had two jobs. I worked full-time at the bank and then worked part-time at this church. I started with such excitement and zeal for the ministry and used all of our free time to do whatever I could to serve the church. But it wasn't too long before we had another blessing. Mandy was to be born. My family was elated, and our church was excited to add a newborn to the nursery. After Mandy was born, I recall a sweet lady who led the nursery coming to the hospital to enroll Mandy in Sunday School.

But as the time progressed, we wanted to have another child. This time Nick would become part of our family. We had moved on to another church and as before everyone we knew celebrated our blessings. My job was progressing, and I was the night manager of operations for this large Northwest bank. Needless to say, our paychecks were getting more substantial just as the cost of living was exploding before our very eyes. I had no idea how much baby food and diapers would be when we started a family. I guess it overwhelmed me so much, I gave both my kids a diaper service for each of their first two kids. These times were tough. It seemed the more I had the more I needed. God was about to test my faithfulness to Him.

I just thought all this nonsense about paying bills and surviving was just that. Survival. I had become dependent on my paycheck to sustain my family. Seems in a few short years, I had forgotten all God did for me when there wasn't enough paycheck to get us through tough times. I lost sight of values for even my family and began to become distant when I couldn't give them the things they wanted. Key emphasis on wanted. We had more than what we needed but it was the wanting curve that started to get my attention. I just wanted to make Barbie as happy as I possibly could. I was so appreciative to have her in my life that I wanted to shower her and the children with gifts of appreciation. Unfortunately, my bank account didn't share that much appreciation.

I would refuse to go to the mall and stay home as I couldn't even face the idea of having to say NO to any of them. Just to hear Barbie speak favorably of anything turned into my wanting to give her what I thought were the desires of her heart. It was just easier to avoid any type of shopping so I wouldn't have to face those situations. Many years later I came to learn it wasn't about the stuff. My family didn't want the stuff. They just wanted to be out and spend time with their husband and father. I really missed out on some good times just because I thought I might have to cover the cost of dinner out when my resourceful wife would have been more than willing to prepare a picnic lunch for the family. Rather than just saying no to them, I started saying no to God.

You're probably thinking, "what an Imbecile!" Well yeah that is kind of what I was. But remember, I am telling this story with hindsight, so it is all clear to me now. Back then I didn't really understand what I was doing even though I knew some of it was not right and didn't honor my God. Not only was I trying to play

God with my family, I was also having issues of faith because I had forgotten who promised to provide for my needs.

Every payday I had the lovely pleasure of sitting down for a couple hours and preparing the bills. We had these things called Checks. I used a check book, envelopes, and stamps to pay my bills. I averaged about forty bills each month to various companies who provided what was needed for my family including my tithe to the church. I got paid twice a month, so I got to do this twenty-four times each year. Barbie left all this money work to me and trusted me to follow our family plan of Christian discipleship. And without her knowledge, I began to fudge the plan just so we could get by.

I remember the first time the notion of not paying the full tithe came to my mind. I thought, I'll just take a little bit of this just to get us by. Before long it was skipping the entire tithe payment to the church just to get by. Not only was I abandoning my trust in God to provide for my family but now I had gone so far as to steal from God. It would have been better had the police come to my home and charged me with grand larceny than what I was about to experience. Just remember as I tell this story, God is always faithful no matter how lost we become along our way. God always provided for my family, but I would find the burden of providing for my family like a heavy weight around my neck.

I started to notice things that had not really happened to me before. I would short the tithe and then my car would require a repair equal to what I had taken from God. I would start to have job challenges that would freak me out thinking my ability to stay employed was about to end. All kinds of unwanted and unexpected things started happening to me which put even more hardship on my young family. But I didn't tell Barb what was really going on. I knew it deep in my soul, but I felt somehow I could pay it back. Even as credit card debt started to add to my load, I just couldn't figure out how to get back on track.

Then it became so obvious to me what was happening. I am thick headed, so God had to break this down for me in very simple terms. I would short the tithe and a car would break down. The repair bill was equal to what I had taken from the tithe. At one point I had three broken cars and had to borrow a vehicle from my extended family just so I could get to work. As I couldn't afford mechanics, I would buy parts and attempt repairs on my own. The parts would then equal what I had shorted on my tithe and the time I lost with my family was spent underneath some greasy leaky vehicle.

God started matching me blow for blow. This went on for months and I just couldn't remain consistent to the obedience of tithing. When I did tithe, nothing would break. But every single time I decided to take some of the tithe, I could count on another trip to the parts store. I absolutely became afraid to even start a vehicle after I had taken from the tithe because I knew what was coming. Dollar for dollar, my foolishness was not getting me ahead in any way. Barb was also puzzled as we had lived a sheltered life and she was starting to wonder why our journey had become so difficult.

Then one day, I realized I couldn't escape this vicious cycle. My decision of robbing from God to get ahead was breaking me and now even hurting my family. God wanted me to get my life back on His path and honor His teachings. The first thing God required was my repentance. I got on my knees and begged God to forgive me. I was no better than a thief. Despite all the blessings I had received from Him, I was ashamed that I had found him untrustworthy. I promised never to again make that decision no matter how bleak the outlook seemed. The next thing God wanted me to do was confess my conduct to Barbie and apologize for putting my family through this hardship. Needless to say, she did not appreciate what I had done and expected me to be obedient to God's precepts and teachings.

Once I had humbled myself and submitted my way to God again, life started to be more joyful. I still faced challenges in those weeks to come but I knew God was testing me to be sure I would be obedient to His commandments. It wasn't too much longer until my employer promoted me again and many of our financial struggles began to go away. The extra money was nice but in my heart, I knew it was never enough without God making a way for us. But when I set my heart and mind on God, once again He started giving my family the true desires of our hearts. Love and joy were abundant in our lives and all of our cars started working reliably once again.

God never needed my tithe. He owned everything. My church never needed my tithe. The church did fine before I showed up and made along even after I moved on. All God wanted was my obedience. In this case the obedience was not for God's own self-actualization or even my own protection. It was to make sure in my heart I understood God provided for me and it wasn't of my own means. Paychecks come and go but God is ever present even in our rebellious times. He never forsakes his faithfulness to provide as he has promised. He also is faithful to teach us the paths of Righteousness. Even if that teaching comes with a quart of oil and a half inch wrench.

I have come to learn there are two times when I can be in the presence of God. At times of worship when I sing praise or pray and seek his words for my life. The other time is when I'm being rebellious. Obviously, I do not prefer these encounters, but I can absolutely say without any doubt that I treasure knowing God cares enough about me to be sure I travel the best path He made for me.

Chapter Six: My Busy Unfruitful Life

I needed clothes and you clothed me, I was sick and you looked
after me, I was in prison and you came to visit me. Matthew 26:36

What do you want from me Lord? That was the question I couldn't escape at this time in my life. Let me be clear, I was about as confused in my spiritual life at this point in my life as I had ever been. I had just resigned serving as an associate pastor because it was clear to me, God never called me to be a pastor. While I loved God's people, deciding to fire the church choir because they were not serious about their commitment to worship, might have been a good clue I was not in the proper lane of service.

From the time I could remember attending church, I was busy about the work of the church. In this I was also seeking a deeper relationship with God and I just couldn't find any contentment in my heart no matter what I was doing at the time. Accepting I had misunderstood my calling to pastoral ministry was just the beginning of my spiritual conflict. By the time I was a teenager I was serving in key roles of the church and leading church programs. I would arrive at church and run as hard as I could go until I completed my list of commitments for that day. If church was open, I was there. I attended Sunday morning and evening services as well as Wednesday evening prayer meetings. I typically had a night for church visitation and usually another day or two for various activities with the church. You had not met many young men who worked harder at what I was doing. Despite all my efforts, I had no peace and I could not find happiness in what I called serving God.

My family life was not in balance either. As you can imagine, I was a young man with a young family who was spending all his time doing anything but being a good dad and husband. It was clearly not creating balance in the home. While I loved my family deeply, I couldn't find a way to make this life plan I had created work for any of us.

Then something snapped. Looking back, I can see the Lord allowed my rubber band to break. I had wound it so tight, it finally snapped. That's when I stopped everything and turned to God and asked for help figuring out what I should be doing with my life. This process turned me inside out. I was asking questions and seeking wisdom from anyone who would talk to me. I had not abandoned my faith in God. I had lost my desire to serve the church. This was critical as I was learning that church busyness is no substitute for the ministry God has put before us. During this time, I questioned everything including the religious structure and practice I had come to accept as religious practices for my life. My wife was more than a bit anxious about me. She had never seen me so confused and disillusioned with life. While I continued to attend church, I was not committed to any roles of service in the church. I stopped attending anything but Sunday morning worship. People who knew me thought I had lost my way. Actually, I was about to unravel exactly what God had been wanting to teach me and the very foundations which would drive my service to God for many years.

I remember the first question I pondered. Why did churches have Sunday evening services and why were they promoting attendance. I couldn't find anything in the Bible about Sunday evening services. Most regular attenders did not attend Sunday evening services. It was only the "most faithful" members who attended on Sunday evening. At least that was the impression

I had gained from being in the inner circle of the church. You might think this was a silly question, but it started the challenge exercise of my view of the church verses serving God. In my research, which happened before the internet was available to tell me everything I wanted to know, I found my answer. Back in the 1800's churches in England who were trying to reach their community with the good news about Jesus had a novel idea. The advent of electric lighting gave churches an idea as to how to get people to come to church to hear the gospel. They decided to have Sunday evening services and turn on the lights. People in their communities flocked to the churches and from this the churches started to grow again. The idea caught on and churches in this country started to follow suit. Thus, the start of Sunday evening church services which eventually morphed into a smaller gathering attached to an even smaller program of Church Training, aka a Sunday evening version of Sunday School. It hit me like a semi when I realized this church practice and now tradition had an amazing start in evangelism. The church was innovating from what they had available, reaching out to people they couldn't otherwise have reached to share the Good News about Jesus. What a practical and appropriate idea. This pushed me to challenge even more about what I had come to accept as religion in my life.

I questioned Baptism, church buildings, church programs, and just about everything else associated with attending church. My sweet and patient wife would watch me spin over every detail. I would ask her these same questions. She wasn't as enamored with the questions as I was. But I always thought she had a wonderful heart for serving God. I really wanted to know more about that happiness right in front of me, but I still couldn't see it. Then I did see it. It had been happening for many years right in front of me. Barbie would find time to bake up a plate of cookies and go visit our older neighbors. She would check on them and pray with them. She would even take our young children with her to brighten that couple's day. Everyone loved Barbie. In fact, people would respond to Barbie's ministry and seek the God she loved.

I still didn't have it figured out, but I started to turn to scripture and found where Jesus spoke to His disciples about ministry. He told them to feed the hungry, visit the sick and imprisoned, to care for the widows and orphans. The Bible was full of instruction for ministry. This ministry was not built around a church program. It didn't require a gathering of members to get anything done. Additionally, I began to understand the work of the early church as they encouraged each other and came together often. They didn't even have large worship centers or church buildings in which to gather. They gathered in homes and hillsides to share their faith with one another. They shared what they had with each other. Then I recognized something most important that would change everything going forward. The world marveled at the Christians in the early church over the way they loved one another. This was the light Jesus wanted to leave behind. Jesus never sought to build up stained glass cathedrals hoping the world would look inside to find him. Instead, He left behind people who wanted to live like Christ and come together within their world and demonstrate what real love was all about. Barb has been showing me what a plate of cookies could do for a world that needed to know God's love. I had been such a fool to think I could be busy about the church and miss the whole point of being a Christian.

Once I started to come out of this spin cycle, I committed myself to live a life of purpose and to server others as Christ has showed us how to do. I was so joyful in my heart that God had snapped my rubber band. While the spin cycle was difficult, I came out of that experience with a better understanding of my ministry going forward and with God's leadership, I was going to become the man God had called me to be. In doing this, I was also going to become a better father, husband, and person. God had a lot of things yet to teach me and He still does. My diamond is still in the rough, but it's actually shaped more like a diamond now than a rock.

I started to push churches to break away from traditions and asked them to think about how they served together. I also challenged them to find new innovations to reach out to others. While electricity was now a main staple in life, it was no excuse to continue to push outdated programs and it was no excuse to become lazy when the world was looking for love. I lacked a lot of experience and know how to move the needle where I was heading next. But what I lacked in experience, I made up for in passion for serving my Savior with a newfound love for His people.

I am so thankful God took the time to redeem my life with His plan. I think back to that twelve year old boy who wanted to answer God's calling on his life but didn't know what else to do but be a preacher. Well, all that time inside the church fishbowl was just what I needed to help those inside look over the side of the bowl with me and seek to step out in a bold new way to follow Jesus in service to the community we had been given. I can't imagine what God thought about me during this time, but I know he never stepped away or left me to find this on my own. He was ever present with me guiding me with His love for the church, His peace for a searching soul, and His teachings which would start to guide my paths. He was always there.

Chapter Seven: ACT One, Uphill Challenge

But I have this against you: You have abandoned your first love. Therefore, keep in mind how far you have fallen. Repent and perform the deeds you did at first. But if you do not repent, I will come to you and remove your candlestick from its place. Revelations 2: 4-5

The church we attended at the time was FBCFW. I choose to refer to church names as abbreviations as to not spread misgivings about any of God's churches. This is not my intention as every church has helped disciple me in a way that has brought me closer to God. This church was about to experience what could happen when God had taken a man like me off spin cycle and put a passion of service into his heart. What was about to happen next could have only happened because God purposed it to happen. Remember, I was young and inexperienced. The only thing I brought to this situation was a big mouth, a big heart and passion with a stubbornness for purpose.

When my family joined this church, it was at the recommendation of my father. The pastor of this church was a really good man and friend of my father's. My dad had also experienced my world being turned inside out and knew I needed a pastor who was up to the task of shepherding a disciple like me. I was all rough around the edges and could only speak in concepts without much authority. This pastor was patient with me and helped me get started in the church. He first asked me to lead their worship. I accepted the offer only with the condition I could lead the church to worship and that did not mean just calling hymn numbers from the church hymnals for singing. He agreed and thus started my first step in this journey.

Sadly, this pastor decided to retire. I was going to miss him even though we had only served together for a short while. As our church sought a new pastor, they extended an invitation to a younger man to lead our church. This new pastor and I connected quickly and I started to push him to help lead our church in a very non-traditional way. I'm still not sure if he was just trying to placate me or if he actually believed in what we were discussing. Nonetheless, this opened doors to test out those concepts God had put in my heart. Our little church was getting smaller. We were down to about fifty people attending on Sunday mornings. We had about twenty there for Sunday evening services and maybe ten or so for Church Training on Sunday evening. As summer was approaching, I encouraged our pastor to abandon our Sunday evening services and stop church training. In its place we would provide a gathering of people from the church in their homes all across our community. People attending on Sunday mornings would take a name from our box which would direct them to a home that Sunday evening. During the evening gatherings several things would occur. There would be time for fellowship together where members of our church got an opportunity to get to know each other. They could share their hearts and connect in service opportunities together. We would also provide a video to be played during this time to challenge our small groups to rise up and become the servants of Christ in our community.

Before my very eyes our church started to grow exponentially. Our Sunday worship services were growing to over two hundred attendees. We were so crowed in that building there was hardly room to find a place to sit down. People who hosted the Sunday evening gatherings were also encouraged to invite their friends and neighbors to their homes. It was not uncommon for these gatherings to have a full house of twenty or so people. Accommodations were made in the home for childcare by the youth of our church who were joining in the ministry. We used to have an alter call during Sunday services and our alter was getting busy. People were committing to the Good News about Jesus. Despite all I had been through as God shook me inside out, I almost couldn't believe how people were responding to the notion of becoming a church that practiced like the early church in the Book of Acts. Once again it just goes to show our Creator knows more about the human condition and His plan for the church than any of the rest of us.

Then like every good thing, The devil shows up and tried to put a stop to all this. It came in the most unexpected way. It came from our new pastor. The pastor felt it was time to stop the home gatherings and return to Sunday evening services and church training. With such a large church that needed discipleship, it was the perfect plan in his mind. Despite my resistance, he took the church back into the traditional religious practices. It wasn't long until we had dropped to about thirty people attending on Sunday morning services. The church was dying a slow and painful death. I couldn't understand why this had to happen.

Before I left the church to find another church that still had a candle stick in its midst, I was able to ask that Pastor why he did what he did. Here's what I learned. When he would attend associational meetings with other pastors and give an attendance report, he would report zero attendance for Sunday evening services and church training. The other pastors would frown upon his choice to abandon the way they had learned to pastor. He finally gave into peer pressure just so he could report attendance. This is where I realized how much passion I had and how little wisdom I had developed. I needed to help a pastor navigate his role as the leader of our congregation. While we were meeting so many needs, we were not addressing his needs. I left saddened that he had missed the greater calling.

Serving with a church who has the candle stick is imperative as a believer. If it's not there, you must search for a fellowship of believers who holds a lit candle stick. Just as Jesus spoke in Revelations to the Church in Ephesus, our church had lost its way and in a moment the light of God was extinguished from our fellowship.

I will remind you again that my purpose for writing this is to demonstrate the presence of God. I was blessed to experience the presence of God's Spirit in this church even though the ending was not what I wanted. Nothing changes people's hearts more than the presence of God's Spirit. Amazing things began to happen in addition to just seeing the church grow numerically. People started using their talents for innovative and impactful ministry. I recall a group of young men who felt compelled to help the widows of our church. They surveyed each lady to learn what model cars they had. They asked about their vehicles operation to learn of any problems. Then on a weekend they scheduled each vehicle into the church parking lot for a no cost tune up and needed repairs. They only did this for the church's widows. When word from these dear ladies got out to their families, children who had forsaken the fellowship of the church, those family members began to show up. The world around us marveled at how they loved one another. Just a simple effort by God's people to care for one another in loving fellowship became a light to our community. It's the modern-day equivalent of finding a way to use electricity to spread the gospel. This was one of many inspired works of God's Spirit amongst our midst. I was hooked. I could never be without this again. While I would struggle to always find it and connect with believers, when God's spirit was present, I was in awe of what could happen.

While act one was now closing, I was learning more about what lay ahead of me. The power to change the status quo was significant. But it was so important that our pastor also own that vision and not just agree to try something different. Lesson learned but I was not broken. God was still calling me to serve, and I just needed to find that next place where I could join other believers in serving God.

Chapter Eight: ACT Two, Sweet Fellowship

They were first called Christians in Antioch. Acts 11:26

I took my family to another church near our home. I tried to convince friends and family we wanted to serve in a church closer to our own home, the reality of having served and failed was heavy on my heart. I had learned much about the power of Christian Fellowship and what could come of it if God's people just came together to share the heart of God within them with others in their church family. I think this is how the Church collectively comes to know the mind of Christ within themselves. As the Bible explains, we are all part of the body. Each of us has a role within the body but the head of the body is Christ. Funny thing about a body is when it is working well, it communicates within itself. Even this parable explains how a foot could boast or a hand could boast of its purpose within the body. That's a huge hint about communication needs within the church. When we show up on Sunday morning for worship time and just a few people are sharing from the platform words to feed our soul, that is not the proper level of communication needed for a church to come together and follow the mind of Christ.

Not too long after we left the Federal Way church, we started attending the GRBC in Auburn Washington. This small congregation met in a small church building not far from our home. I had hoped to get to know people by connecting in ministry which would lead to connecting with many other people in our neighborhood. It wasn't long before I started asking questions again and stirring up things amongst the congregation. I started asking the same questions to them that I had already asked myself to move out of the rut I had been in for most of my life. When the word of God is put out there in a question or challenge to another brother in love, the Holy Spirit will start to chip away at their hearts just like He had done with my own.

It wasn't long before the pastor took a lead to reimagine how we could better serve our purpose in the community we were in. I jumped on that wave with him. God's spirit began to move people and before long that small church building was busting at the seams. People had a genuine affection for each other which had come from simply spending more time with each other in homes and serving in our community. I made some very good friends at this church. In fact, my wife encouraged a family about our age not far from our home with children about our kids age to come to the church with us. It wasn't just a single invitation but a relationship and friendship that grew between us. Before long the love of our God had reached their hearts and they began to reconsider what God meant to them. The couple Barb invited to the church now leads an amazing program teaching Christ to the Jewish people and helping them understand how the law and the feast and the teaching of the Old Testament were fulfilled in Christ and are still relevant today. I was humbled recently when the Cathcart's visited us while passing thru Spokane. They shared memories of times many years ago when we served and worshiped God together. They thanked us for our fellowship with them as it was a turning point in their own lives. I didn't know what to say other than glory to our God who knew how to bring us together in the body so we can all go about fulfilling our purpose.

Many things happened at this church while we were there. One of the more innovative things we did for the community was to hold a church Olympics. It was one of those years when the summer Olympics were being held somewhere. So in the spirit of community and competition, we decided to invite anyone who wanted to participate to join us on a Sunday afternoon for Church Olympics. We divided into four teams. I remember being one of the team captains. We did all kinds of silly activities to compete for the prize which was mainly bragging rights as the winning team. One of the events was an eating contest. Eating has always been one of my more advanced life skills. The captains were to eat several things including onions and various other nasty plates prepared for this event. My team was in second place to my good friend Tim. Up next was a plate of bananas. I knew we could both finish that plate of bananas. So being the sharp and crazy man that I was, I challenged my friend Tim to double the points if finishing the bananas included one banana with the peel. He agreed and the contest proceeded. We both chewed through that banana peel. Was that banana peel chewy. It had at least one thousand percent of the daily recommended dosage of fiber. Not only was it difficult going down but digestion was not pleasant either. To this day, I believe it likely was the reason I got early onset to Diverticulitis. When the doctor did my exam, he said I had the colon of a man twenty years older than I was. All I could think about at that time was the impact of the banana peel. I may have won the event which allowed our team to get the gold medal, but I paid for that proud moment the rest of my life. If only I could have been more humble. Kind of reminded me of Moses striking the rock. He got his moment of fame, but he didn't win the long game. Despite this I still remember this day fondly as new people came to our congregation just from playing a silly game.

In the midst of all this happiness and amazement of God's working amongst our church, I still had something important God needed to teach me. This next lesson would be painful but something life changing which was going to sustain me in moments of trial and faith for years to come. The bank I worked for had been sold and there was great uncertainty about my future employment status. Looking back, I cannot even get my head around the fear I had in my heart at that time. I had a young family to care for and couldn't imagine how that would be possible without a paycheck. But God knew exactly how that was going to be possible. I just needed to get to a point in my life where I was ready to learn how God provides and what He expects from me.

One afternoon during my drive home from work, I started to cry out to God to spare my family from hardship. I acknowledged that while I was attempting to live a Godly life, I did not have a strong faith. I begged God to help me and help my faith not waiver during this time. That's when God started getting busy in my life. First, the company announced it would triple the severance to any employee let go during this upcoming merger. With eleven years with this company that gave me 33 weeks of income to help me make a transition. Then other companies started calling me to interviews. I would go talk to them and when I came back my company continued to raise my severance to the point I had two and a half years committed salary to cover my family wellbeing. I went from hoping to find a job in this merger to hoping I could be laid off and start life anew with this severance from the bank. That's exactly what happened. Immediately following the layoff, I got a consulting job that funded another six months of living. Because I was in a layoff, I also got unemployment pay for the time I was seeking employment. Anyone else would look at this situation and think, there is nothing to worry about and God stood behind His commitment to provide for my needs. But I was not satisfied. I was still desperate to find employment. Rather than enjoying a well-deserved rest with my family, I started a job search hoping to find anyone who wanted to pay for my services.

The calls from companies stopped. For months, I would send out resumes, connect with associates in the industry yet nothing was moving. While I had more than enough put away for employment transition, the longer this dragged on, the more I worried my savings would be used up and there would be nothing left to provide for my family. I was very focused on economizing every dollar and spending all my time in this job search. Then I started running out of places to call and positions to consider. Rather than go to the outplacement center and job search, I just stayed home wasting time with worry. God had had enough of my childlike behavior and was about to show himself to me in an amazing way.

Our church building had a basement and it flooded. The cleanup work was significant and needed someone to manage the restoration. God told me to stop looking for work and do this project for the church. God and I had a long discussion about my priorities, but He was very firm on his position as to what I should be doing with my time. Additionally, I began to recognize other people who needed a bit of assistance and I was available to serve them with my time. I found joy again in my soul as I was busy about my Father's work. Somewhere along the way, God set me down and made it very clear to me how much He loved me and His promise to provide for me was something I could trust. He also clarified another important lesson for me. I was made to work and serve God. I had always associated working with a way to secure God's provision for my family. But the two things have nothing to do with each other. In fact, by accepting my responsibility to work as God had created for me to do, I was fulfilling God's ordinance in my life. I was also recognizing God was going to provide as long as I obeyed Him and put my faith in His promises. This is clearly not the way the world sees the path to financial security. However, it is God's path to success and happiness.

I have been tested many times as to whether or not I really trusted God's promise to provide. This experience of learning to do godly work even if it was for an employer was all I was ever required as a man to do towards trusting in God's provision. Companies have wanted to dismiss me many times. I have even suggested they do so just to see if God had something else for me to do. I never really feared again for God's provision for my family. God's presence in this trial built true Godly character. I would never look at work or God's ability to provide the same again.

Having cherished this sweet fellowship with my church family and the opportunity to walk with God, it was time for our family to take a big step of faith and move to the next big thing in life. It was a sad day when I had to say goodbye to my church and my friends there. I realized the church was growing because of the sweet fellowship within itself. The love we had for one another was noticed by the world around us as we participated in ministry together. People wanted to belong to the church because God's light was shining bright.

I took another job with a company which would be moving me to Denver. It was the company of which I would ultimately finish my employment career. It was still hard to go. What an experience to see God's presence alive and working within His people when the local shepherd was also eager to care for the flock as the Spirit led. I was eager to reconnect with yet another church fellowship and participate as the Spirit of God led. I didn't know anyone in Denver, but I was going to find God's people. What a turnaround God was already doing in my life since He took me off spin cycle. I was starting to realize my real purpose in life. I was beginning to see my role was to assist pastors and leaders to follow where the Spirit was leading even if that meant taking us off the traditional path. What I had witnessed God do, had changed me forever. I believe God was still preparing me for the next thing. I was eager and excited to find what was ahead of us.

Chapter Nine: Act Three, Maybe I'm Not Supposed to be Here

I know your deeds, your hard work and your perseverance. I know that you cannot tolerate wicked people, that you have tested those who claim to be apostles but are not, and have found them false. You have persevered and have endured hardships for my name, and have not grown weary. Yet I hold this against you: You have forsaken the love you had at first. Consider how far you have fallen! Repent and do the things you did at first. If you do not repent, I will come to you and remove your lampstand from its place. Revelation 2: 2-5

I have to say, working with a church start up and a small growing church is a lot of work. It can wear a body down. When I got to Denver, I had the bright idea it was time to go find a mega church and learn more about how a growing church was operating. So, we found the biggest church in Denver whereby we had likeminded beliefs. I am going to call this church FBD.

My new job was challenging me in more ways that I had ever expected possible. There was so much to do and so little time to get it done if we were going to salvage this business. While I had been told this was a strong viable business, when I got my first profit-loss statement for the month, we had recorded $250,000 in revenue and also recorded $500,000 in expenses. This was nowhere near a profitable business. As I got into this project, I began to see the people who put this acquisition model together did not fully understand how to project cost for commercial banking operations and had grossly underestimated the cost of operations. The folks at corporate were starting to wonder what kind of goofball they had hired to run their Denver business and made it clear these loses were not acceptable. Over the next eleven months, our team pulled together and turned that monthly loss into a $2,000 profit. It was not easy on anyone, and I didn't even know what free time was like anymore. I say all this to help you understand why I hoped to hide away in a mega church and let the Lord carry me for a while.

God had different plans for me. While I was not prepared to accept any big commitments to the church while my personal schedule was overtaxed, I couldn't help but feel that same longing in my heart to bear witness as to what God could do with a people who loved their God and would be willing to follow Him. I remember after attending this new church for a few weeks, I kept feeling lost. Not just because the building was massive and navigating thru the maze was a challenge but because people were running all the time. I would try to say hello to someone in the hallway and most the time they would explain how much they would like to visit but they were on their way to some committee meeting or some other busy things the church was doing. Barb had agreed to help with the children as she always loved to do. One Sunday between Sunday School and worship services she asked me to step into the nursery for just a moment to watch the babies so she could run to the restroom. There was no one else there yet and she had been waiting for some time. I agreed and off she went. Then the director of the nursery program whom I had met several times demanded to know who I was and why I was alone unauthorized with all these babies. While I appreciated the need for caution, I was stunned at the sharp rebuff and the lack of recognition or consideration for being a fellow member of the church.

After Barbie returned from the restroom, she saved my hide as I think this woman was going to call the police on me. I then asked the woman why she didn't remember me as she saw me every Sunday when I walked Barbie to the nursery. She tried to make excuses and apologize but warned me never to enter the nursery again. Somewhere in all the business of serving the people in this church had lost their way. They were way more invested in programs than people. I began to ask questions to people in my Sunday School class about the way of their church and if in fact we were following Christ by supporting all this busyness. The words started to speak to others, and they also began asking questions about the effectiveness of their ministry in the church. As a small group we began to gather mid-week together for prayer and fellowship. Before long this small Sunday School class of ten young married couples began to grow. Soon we were joined by fifty people and required a larger room on Sundays for our gathering. My conviction to follow God was not intended to be a revolution but rather a challenge to reconsider why we were here and what we should be doing besides being busy at the church.

This church had so many resources and our group was interested in putting some of that to work. I learned this church had several millions of dollars sitting in the bank which was being used to grow their investment value. A church this large did not support any single mission activity nor any community outreach effort. People in Denver were needing the Good News and we were debating if the carpet in the worship center needed to be replaced. Clearly the illusion of church had been lost on FBD. This was nothing like the church in the Bible, there was a growing set of members within the congregation wanting to do more than just be busy about the programs within. I was not the only person asking questions. This spirit within the congregation was alive and growing. Growing in such a way the senior pastor had heard about us and was wanting to meet with me. He had determined in his research, I was the person that showed up when things started to change. When he asked to come to my home, I was so excited to meet him as I had hoped to reach out to him and partner is this new work God was trying to do.

The pastor arrived at our home, and he started to ask me about my activity within the church. I shared my passion for ministry with fellow believers and believed God was ready to do a great work within the fellowship of FBD. The pastor on the other hand had been sent there by the church leadership to stop the noise so the church could return to the way it was. I learned quickly people were feeling very uncomfortable with the change that was underway and they wanted it to stop. The pastor asked me why I felt it was my responsibility to lead a revolution within his church? I was shocked. I had never considered anything I had done to be unwanted as I assumed every believer wanted to have a bright light of Christ beaming from within their midst. He then suggested there was another church not far from where I lived on the east planes of Denver that might be a better fit for me. Yep, I had been asked to leave. I mean they were hoping I never returned and would go to this new church the following Sunday. Somehow, I knew this is what I needed to do so I thanked the pastor and said my goodbyes.

A few people from FBD reached back for me to find out what had happened to my family but honestly not that many. I gathered now that I was out of their way, things really did start to go back to the way they were before as no one really wanted to rock the boat.

The new church which I'll call EPBC, was a short but amazing experience. All that I had hoped to learn from FBD, I was really going to learn from EPBC. We were not at this church long. After I led my team to fix the business, my company asked me to take a new role leading their western region operations. This new role would move my family to San Diego. The few months at EPBC were some of the most useful months of learning about God's design for joyful service I had ever experienced since God and I went on spin cycle.

The church met in a high school auditorium. Their attendance was around two hundred people and they were growing daily. They were looking for a place to build a church building but that was not their greater mission. Their mission was focused on fellowship, discipleship and evangelism while ministering and worshiping together. The church had many small groups who were very active. The small groups had a loving fellowship and we immediately felt like we belonged and had a family. Further, these small groups did ministry together. It was truly one of the most amazing uses of small groups I had ever witnessed. The jobs within the church no one ever liked to do were not assigned to individuals but to small groups. There was a group assigned to Sunday set up, tear down, greeting, children's church, nursery, and the Sunday treats with coffee to be served before services. We never had a day when there was not enough people to support these activities. Couples did children's church and nursery duty together. It wasn't just the women. We all pitched in. Guys were not intimidated to work with the children because they knew their buddies were going to be on the floor with them helping with the little ones. We actually looked forward to doing this together. Every week before our small group would dismiss, the leader would tell us which duty was assigned to our group and we all looked forward to doing that work together.

I was in amazement at what God was doing in this church. For the very first time, I felt the experience I was having with my church was exactly what God had always intended for His church. People in our community were drawn to us because we truly loved one another. It was an absolutely beautiful thing. I was sad to leave more than anyplace I had ever served because I wanted to learn more about how to be a member in this type of fellowship. But, we were heading to San Diego and with great appreciation for the short time we were there and the great learning we had experienced, we knew God had something even better for us in San Diego. So, my company packed us up and moved us to a little community in east San Diego county called Alpine. This was to be our home for the next fourteen years. We had no idea what was ahead of use but as always, trusting God for the next big thing.

Chapter Ten: Act Four, On Deck

When the three companies blew the trumpets and broke the pitchers, they held the torches in their left hands and the trumpets in their right hands for blowing, and cried, "A sword for the LORD and for Gideon!" Each stood in his place around the camp; and all the army ran, crying out as they fled. When they blew 300 trumpets, the LORD set the sword of one against another even throughout the whole army; and the army fled. Judges 7: 20-22

How does someone even tell such a story of God's presence in our lives. There are so many cliches that come to mind as I start this story. The first is so overused but very appropriate. Hindsight is twenty-twenty. When the Bible speaks of Jesus completing a good work in you, you can be sure it's a journey. If I had the good sense to look at what God was doing with me, it was clearly a lifetime of preparation for a time in service for Him. I say journey because God seldom does anything as simple as connecting two dots to get you where He wants you. When God is completing a good work in you, it typically involves a broad plan of interactions working with each other to bring about something only He could accomplish lest we boast or attempt to take credit for what he has done. It was clearly time for me to be "On Deck". I had been at the practices and played in the minor leagues but now it was my time to participate in God's work in a way that humbles me to this very day.

Another cliche maybe not so overused is one of my favorites. I was once asked, "If you could do anything to accomplish something wonderful without fear of failure or repercussion, what would you do?" While this was a great axiom for the business world it is exactly how God expects faith to function in our lives. The question is truly about faith in God's greatness and not our own abilities. When that moment comes to step into the realm of God's Majesty and bear witness and speak as his own child with strength and courage, will you do it? I suspect you're thinking, of course I will. Be careful before you speak because God will put you in a situation whereby your actions will look like foolishness to all men, and you will be left vulnerable and possibly somewhat deemed ridiculous when you speak out in faith.

So now to the story. We had just moved to San Diego County as my job relocated me to a bigger role within my company. I was to hold the role of Chief Operating Officer for the Western Region of our business. It was a big responsibility, and I was only certain of one thing, I was not qualified to be in this job. However, God had bigger plans than this job for me. It was really all about getting me into our new home located in Alpine California. Alpine was a smaller town located in east San Diego County just at the foothills before you entered what we called the high desert. Nestled in this beautiful community would be a place we would call home for the next fourteen years of our lives. I had a job and a home. All I needed next was to find my church.

Given the prior experiences I shared about my prior churches, I wanted to steer clear of any big churches in the area as I did not want to repeat my former experience. I was much more cautious this time as I also did not want to push for a change to a church but rather join a fellowship with a bright Candle Stick, shining for all the community to see. So, we looked around and quickly realized our little town of Alpine did not offer very many options for church. We would drive around the community looking for church buildings in attempts to find our new church fellowship. There were only a couple of protestant churches in the entire town. One of them was definitely not going to work as the gap in our theology was too great for a comfortable fellowship. The other was interesting, but something just did not feel right as we attended worship with them. I was puzzled as to what I should do next and then I saw an office building for a church I will refer to as ACF. It was a small office in a professional building that did not look big enough to hold a church gathering of any kind. I suspect if ten people gathered there, half of them would have to stand in the doorway.

I dismissed ACF because I could not see anything in the way of evidence a true church fellowship was active there. Then one day I decided to drive up to the office building and inquire to the administrative assistance, just what was the deal with ACF. This sweet lady, who would become a treasured friend, started to tell me all about her church. Then she shared about their vision of ministry to the Alpine community. Finally, she shared a bit of information about the church's history. I learned this was a new church start up and they were meeting in a middle school gym for Sunday services. I hope that I am not the only one starting to see the pattern here. Our family visited the church and fell in love with the people there and soon decided this was to be our church home. We were right back at setting up chairs every Sunday for services and gathering in homes and community centers together as we had opportunities to fellowship.

I was enjoying the experience and my family was connecting with others in the church to find fulfillment in their own lives. I remember meeting a dear couple we connected with shortly after arriving at ACF. Roy and Joanne were their names. Roy was a fun guy and had a twisted sense of humor like I did. Our first residence in Alpine was a rental house with a large yard. Part of my tenant duty was to care for the yard and gardens. I purchased a riding mower to assist with the lawn care. On one side of this property there was a large gulch. The hill down to the gulch was part of the yard which had to be mowed. The hill was fairly steep, so I used great caution when taking the mower down the hill. Actually, taking that mower down the hill required a skilled maneuver at the bottom of the hill to quickly turn right or you would drop off into the gulch filled with chaparral and likely rattlesnakes. I had little interest in meeting any of the residents of the gulch, so I took the sharp turn defying the speeds of gravitational pull driving me into the gulch with hopes I did not roll the mower over the cliff in the process. The first couple of passes were always the most challenging as the slope higher and the space to turn was much smaller. Pondering this problem, I decided it might be simpler to go up the hill instead. I was not certain the mower would pull me up the hill, but anything sounded better than this nerve crushing experience of taking that mower down the suicide hill every weekend. So, I started the mower up the hill one Saturday morning. It was handling the climb just fine as I had purchased the larger engine for this machine. I had also purchased the type of mower where the engine mounted in the rear of the mower with the driver's seat mounted just in front of the engine. Having a life long history of not thinking things through, I should have anticipated what was going to happen. The front of the mower started to roll up on me and before I knew it, I was under the mower with it still running full speed on top of me. I was still seated with the blade running full power above my body with the exception that the weight of the machine was crushing me into the slope of that nasty hill. I reacted with great strength as the panic I was experiencing obviously told my body to throw this mower as far away from me as I could muster. So that is just what I did. Fortunately, it rolled away from me, and the blade stopped. The mower appeared to have no damage. I appeared to have all my body parts still connected where they belonged. As I shared this story with the guys at church the next day, my friend Roy, could not stop laughing. After church was over after and we arrived home; my buddy Roy shows up in his work truck. He had shown up with one inch steel tubing and a welder as he was prepared to add a roll cage to my mower. Very funny. Although I drove a mower like I was part of NASCAR, I was not prepared to retrofit a mower in hopes I would ever roll a vehicle again. I had just decided to let the grass grow on the hill and buy a house as soon as we could make that happen. This is why I fell in love with the people at ACF. It was never a dull moment there.

Again, in my efforts to learn from my past experiences, I chose to take a passive role in the church. I was happy to do whatever I could, but I wanted to grow with the church and not attempt to refocus the church in any way. Despite my efforts to keep a low profile, God had other plans for me. Before long, the pastor asked me to join the Elder Board and help lead this church in the work God had for our community. Honestly, I was reluctant to accept but there was no doubt in my heart this was to be my calling. A lifetime of living and experiencing God's presence was about to put me "on deck" and to follow God where He was leading us.

The church was growing, and the Lord was blessing in so many ways. The school district who loved our money for renting their facilities each week also forced a big change in our plans as a church. We had one year and then we were going to have to stop using their facilities unless we could prove we had long term plans for another property to use for gathering our church fellowship. Talk about a wrinkle in our plans. Everything was going along quite well and then we had to turn to God for a way out of this problem. First, we considered any other facility we could use in the community. Nothing else was available that could support a church our size. We were averaging about a hundred people each week at services. Clearly, we had moved beyond small, but we were far from big enough to purchase anything due to the high cost of southern California real estate. The search had to begin for a place we would call our own. The elders met and prayed for God's direction, and everything looked impractical if not impossible.

I served on this board with some of God's chosen men. We were an interesting bunch of guys you could have ever contemplated working together. I don't think anyone would have assembled a group like this one except for one common thing, we loved God, and we loved His church with all our hearts. Each man on this board brought something unique. My dear brother, John, was the chairman of this board. He and I bonded close together as we undertook this challenge of finding a new church home. John and I would talk and pray frequently. John recognized my purpose on the board and the church even more than I could. As we continued the search it soon became clear there were two parcels of land just off the freeway that would be ideal for our church home. The parcels were owned by two different sellers. The first was a two and a half acre parcel adjacent to the offramp of the freeway. This parcel was selling for $250,000. The adjacent parcel was thirteen acres, and it was selling for $1.3 million. That meant our church would somehow need to come up with just over $1.6 million dollars to acquire the property and pay all the purchase fees.

The board gathered in prayer and discussion about the purchase. I was always the guy with all the questions. I had questions because I wanted to be certain I understood just how impossible this was without a miracle from God. As we reviewed our funds and contemplated the possibility of a mortgage, we were all certain based on our own math, we would default on the loan before closure and lose our escrow payment of $25,000. None-the-less, with absolute certainty we all agreed to move forward with a purchase offer and begin the process of acquiring this amazing property for the Lord's church at ACF.

There was much to do as we had to prepare site plans, get permits and approvals from various agencies before we could actually begin building anything on the site. The work was demanding. My dear brother John carried much of the workload. He was a contractor by trade and his skill set was just what God wanted to help us find our way through this maze of activities we were about to begin. The site plan included a ten year building plan which repurposed an old house on the thirteen acre parcel to be used for the new church office. It also included an initial worship center and plans for a much larger worship center which would eventually be needed to accommodate the growth of the church. As we approached the final steps of the permitting process so we could complete the sale, we had to get the California EPA involved to clear the property of any hazards. Oddly enough the timing of this event was delayed a bit. We had hoped to get through all this work before our second escrow payment was due. That did not happen as planned. John called me and asked me what I thought we ought to do. I told John with great confidence we needed to send another $25,000 to escrow to hold this property while we finished the permitting process. I knew this was the place God wanted us to be so there was no doubt in my mind we needed to keep the sales process open while the state finished their work. Besides, the very next day the state EPA was showing up for their inspection so why did we even need to stop and pray about this.

Late the next day I got a call from John. He was very troubled and asked me to meet him at the church office. I immediately left home to meet him there. He shared the news. The state EPA inspector had found an issue. He was certain he had finally found that long lost illegal dumping site right underneath the property we were going to purchase. This was being described as a massive cleanup site if anything were ever to be built on the property. A methane test was to be ordered if we were to proceed. Likely, the building we built would require vapor barriers to protect from any methane gases once we had removed all the trash and backfilled with clean dirt. My heart sank. We had just sent that $25,000 escrow payment without consulting with the board or with God. There was no way we could continue the building plans as we knew them because the cost of a cleanup was mandatory and would be conducted by the state then billed to the church. I suggested to John we gather the board for an emergency meeting to discuss what had happened and to seek their forgiveness regarding the escrow payment while asking God for guidance.

The board gathered the very next evening as we contemplated next steps. Some were so discouraged they were ready to walk away from the entire plan and start looking for property again. We were like chickens without our heads. Our pastor called for prayer. We joined together in prayer and in that prayer time, God started speaking to me. He reminded me how he had brought our church to this property. He had already claimed it for the church. The only problem we had was to consider how God wanted to redeem this land for His church. God knew what we could not see. He saw many people coming to this church and coming to know Jesus as their personal Savior and Lord. He saw all the ministry to people who had needs that would be met at this church for many years to come. He could see all of this ahead of us but first he had to get this rag tag group of men to remember who was making these plans.

At the end of the prayer, I timidly started to challenge the men as God had been speaking to me. I asked them how we were so certain this was God's plan for our church just a few days ago and now we were ready to turn tails and run for shelter just because this looked even more impossible. God continued to push me to find the impossible. I asked John to get out the site plan to draw over it where the inspector had determined the landfill to be located on the properties. John drew a large shape over the site plan that covered about twenty-five percent of the land. Most of the shape covered the 2.5-acre parcel but continued in a triangular fashion into the 13-acre parcel. Immediately, I knew part of God's plan never really included the 2.5-acre parcel. I had always kind of known this as we aspired to have corner access to the freeway so we could better advertise our property to the community. I first asked John if we could consider eliminating the 2.5-acre parcel from our plot plan. He acknowledged the plan could be modified. It got me to wondering if we could move the buildings around enough to put parking lots over the dump sites and position buildings over clean soil. John made cutouts of the various buildings for the plot design. We started a process of moving pieces around the 13-acre parcel like we were group solving a big puzzle. None of our ideas seemed likely to work despite our persistence to find a plot design that might pass inspection. Fundamentally, everything came down to one important question.

Would we continue with the methane test or just turn the property back to the investor group who owned the land?

God spoke to me one more time and this time. In my soul a wildly bizarre plan was manifesting itself to me. It was so crazy I dared not share it with anyone or they might think I had lost my mind. God reminded me again of my purpose in this work and to trust His plan and not try to rationalize any of this. Here's what God asked me to do. He wanted me to ask the sellers if they would be willing to sell this property to the church for the money we had in escrow plus pay the back taxes of $10,000. If they would accept the offer, we would take full responsibility for site cleanup and relieve them of any further responsibility to the site. I wasn't sure if escrow was to have $25,000 or $50,000 as we were trying to stop the cashier's check that had just been sent for the second escrow payment. The men looked at me like I had lost my mind. For once they were right. I was not in my right mind but rather following the Spirit of God speaking to me. I began an attempt to convince these men we are compelled to finish the work that God started on this property. I wasn't sure if we could ever build a church there or not. I actually suggested at some point we might have to operate a golf driving range if we couldn't build there. I didn't know how but I knew for certain God wanted us to make this ridiculous offer to the investors and allow God to put his fear in their hearts so they would turn the land title over to the church.

After a brief discussion, every man there agreed this was so ridiculous it must be of God. I then turned to John and asked if we could get our sales consultant on the line before we adjourned so we could instruct him on next steps while everyone was there to hear the conversation. Since I had been doing most of the talking to that point, our pastor asked if I would be willing to share our strategy with the consultant. At first the consultant asked me if I had lost my mind. Since that seemed to be the theme of the evening, I took no offense to his jaded remarks. Then he refused to make the offer as he said it wasn't even a professional consideration worth his reputation. But then I reminded him he was under contract to represent our church, and this is the offer we wanted to make. He reluctantly agreed to reach out to the nine separate investors the next day with the offer. It took a couple of days, but the call came from John. He said, "Bill, you're never going to believe this, but the investors were all relieved to be rid of this high-risk cleanup project they couldn't wait to close escrow and accept our offer." I completely believed it but still was shocked and humbled at how God had made this happen.

There was still much to be completed. The board gathered again and we discussed proceeding with the methane testing knowing if we failed the test a mandatory clean up would be required. We could not stop the escrow check and we prayed that money would be recovered somehow but expected the sale to close accordingly. I then suggested we contact the owner of the 2.5-acre property to see if he would split the cost of the methane test with the church. He agreed even though the church had most of the testing which had to be conducted across our much larger acreage. We prayed and awaited the measurement day for the methane readings. I was so anxious about the results I took a day off work to join John, our pastor and the inspector at the site for the reading from the drilled sites. The first reading was from the 2.5-acre parcel. The methane readings were very high and clearly were not suitable for use without a major site cleanup. The drilling had uncovered decaying trash which was the source of the methane. During the early process of taking land possession, the church has put up a fence around the 13-acre parcel. As the inspector climbed over the fence, you could see the joy on his face as he knew he had discovered a major environmental site cleanup project for the state. He approached the nearest gauge about twenty yards east of the gauge on the other parcel which read high readings of methane. The look on that inspector's face was priceless. His smile turned to puzzlement when he found no methane readings from the church's drill site. He quickly moved to other drill sites and again found no evidence of methane anywhere on the property the church now owned. I will never forget his final comment of disbelief, "All of these gauges read absolutely no evidence of methane. Honestly with this many men standing in such proximity to the gauges, one would think it could at least register some methane." I guess it was a good thing we all ate healthy lunches before we came to the site. The three of use turned to each other knowing we had just witnessed a miracle from God. Had we not exited the 2.5-acre parcel we would be involved in that clean up. How it was possible to not have any methane was clearly an act of God. We stopped, worshiped, and gave glory to the Father for the good things He had done.

A few months passed and we planned a site cleanup day for the property. Everyone was busy working to get the site ready to start remodeling the office for relocation onto the property. I remember one of our members going into the dirt cellar below the office and bringing out several very large rattlesnakes. Gave me the shivers. But not as big of shivers as to what was going to happen next. One of the women in the church tripped over a piece of rebar sticking up from the ground and asked me to help dig it out of the dirt so no one else would trip or be injured. As I dug, I began to realize this rebar was attached to something much larger. It was attached to asphalt and much more rebar in the ground. There was a dump site below us, and we had found it. The most amazing thing we found was the rebar had a stamp on it that read "State of California". This dump site had been used by the state to destroy the old highway so they could install Interstate 8. John and I could not wait to call the inspector to tell him the news of a required clean up and we even knew who was responsible for the cleanup. Just like that the cleanup for the site started. The state dug out all of their old trash and replaced it with beautiful clean soil.

Six months later I got another call from John who was working at the church office. He had just received a call from our bank letting us know that $25,000 cashier's check had never been deposited by the escrow company. The check was now stale dated, and they wanted to know if we wanted to reissue a replacement check or have the funds returned to our account. If there was any doubt God was attending to every detail of this land purchase, it was removed for me in that moment. I told John we would likely see that lost check again someday when we got to heaven and God showed us his museum of miraculous artifacts to include the Ark of the Covenant and such things.

How can you not see God's presence at work amongst our small church at ACF. The elders decided to share this story with the congregation as we started to undertake the next steps to build our worship center. I was blessed to have the honor of getting to share the story from beginning to end with the congregation. They were as amazed as we all were to hear how God put His fear in the hearts of the investors right down to returning the lost escrow check. ACF was here because God and God alone wanted us to be where we were that day. We had a great calling and purpose for which we would forever be blessed and forever responsible for sharing the Gospel from this sacred place.

I left that church after almost fourteen years of service. It was hard to go but I knew God had another chapter in my life still unwritten. I still long sometimes just to go back to visit ACF to see if they still remember what God did there so many years ago to establish His church in Alpine California. I do know before I left the church the growth there was amazing. The church's ministry was far reaching, and God was completing a good work in all of us.

Chapter Eleven: Brown Bagging Wildfires

The harvest is plentiful, but the laborers are few; therefore pray earnestly to the Lord of the harvest to send out laborers into his harvest. Matthew 9: 37-38

Most people think about the fear of earthquakes when they live in southern California. I remember the anxiousness I had about earthquakes just before relocating to San Diego. Lucky me, I had several remote offices across California including Los Angeles area and San Francisco which I considered the hot bed for most of the big quakes. In fact, after taking responsibility for my new role, I learned of the big earthquake in Northridge where we also had a remote office. The manager of that location was missing for a couple days as her refrigerator fell over and blocked the apartment door. She couldn't get out until after she was rescued. I think this all occurred within a couple weeks of my new job duties. Talk about an abrupt learning curve about how to manage emergency situations, I got a crash course, no pun intended. At that point in time, I still had not personally experienced an earthquake. The experience eluded me until I started working remotely at an office I had in east Los Angeles. It was a large data center and I had a nice front corner office there. I had several managers who ran the operations, and I was there to make sure our larger consolidation plans were being managed effectively. Shortly after my arrival, I was sitting in my office when it happened. Oh yeah, the room started shaking and the large windows on my south wall started to rattle. I immediately did what I had always been taught to do in such a situation. I ducked under my large steel desk and took cover until I knew it was safe to come out. I stayed there a bit after the shaking stopped and then carefully backed out of the desk to pull myself up to assess the damage. I could not see any immediate damage. When I glanced at the office doorway, I did find several of my managers standing in a huddle wondering where I had gone. To their amusement as I appeared from underneath the desk, they asked if I was alright and tried to assure me everything was fine. This had only been a small 4.8 magnitude earthquake and there was no need for such a reaction. Clearly there was a big difference in how native Californians reacted to earthquakes verses a newbie like me.

While I eventually adjusted to the periodic rumbling of the earth, nothing ever felt good about the sound of those Santa Anna winds as they started sweeping in from the coastline towards the high desert as the cold air moved in to displace the warmer desert air. These winds could reach hurricane force. The sounds of the wind blowing outside my home was eerie as it whistled around the walkways and through the trees. The force of the winds would slam the house like someone had crashed a semi-truck into the side of the house at high speed. While this was happening and everyone was watching the news and hoping they didn't lose power, deep down inside our thoughts, there was this fear some dufus was going to start a brushfire and the winds would sweep the fire thru the county like ocean waves smashing the beachhead. The feeling was almost evil as it was like Satan was roaming the earth seeking what he could devour. Of course, there was always someone who either intentionally or unintentionally would get a fire started. Sometimes it was a cigarette butt thrown out the car window. Other times, it was someone striking a match to watch what they could burn. No matter how much the news would call for caution, someone would always do something to get those fires started. The most we could hope for is that someone did not leave a fire anywhere close to where we were.

Once there was a man who started a fire unintentionally by firing a shotgun into the air because he was lost and attempting to locate his hunting buddy. The hot pellets from the buckshot fell to the ground and the chaparral started to burn. The winds caught that small fire and turned it into the largest fire ever to hit San Diego County. This fire would burn for weeks as the winds were relentless with no end in sight. The summer had been extra hot and everything on the ground was kindling to drive the fire onward. The first night of the windstorm, I was awakened to things blowing around in my yard. In fact, Barb and I had to go out to the back yard and secure the pool furniture, so it didn't blow through a window. It was at that time we realized our daughter was not home. She had gone on a date and was supposed to be home by eleven. I had not heard about a fire starting yet but I was very aware of the windstorm. I tried calling for my daughter, but she didn't answer. Barb and I became very concerned as we assumed she had tested our curfew rules again. By the time she rolled up at 2:00 a.m., I was consumed with anger over her failure to check in and be home on time. She kept trying to make excuses suggesting there was a large fire down the freeway and the firemen were not allowing people to head east towards our home. I assumed it was just a big excuse and put her to bed as we all attempted to unwind so we could get some sleep before getting to church on Sunday morning.

By Sunday morning I began to realize I had been unfair with our daughter as the news of the firestorm was starting to be broadcast on the news channels. I attempted to make amends and assured her I was glad she got home safely. The winds kept howling and signs of that firestorm we beginning to feel uncomfortably close to home. While the firestorm was still at least 15 to 20 miles away, everyone needed to be mindful as these storms could move quickly with those powerful Santa Anna winds pushing them with gust exceeding 70 mph.

As we got to church that morning, I gathered with the other board members to discuss the situation. By this time, the fire had reached a neighboring town and was moving southeast towards the town of Alpine. Many people had come to morning services to join in prayer for the safety of their friends and family. We decided to proceed with the services. I was to keep watch towards the northwest ridge about three miles away for any signs of the firestorm. We all agreed should we see the fire top that ridge, we should vacate the church property immediately to give everyone time to exit as we only had a single road leading off the property to the freeway and surrounding roads as a safety exit. Towards the end of the morning service, I saw the fire come up over the ridge. The winds were strong, and smoke was covering the skyline. I signaled for to our pastor to close the service and ask everyone to depart. Our pastor called the ushers to take the offering before we departed and then closed in prayer. Prayer, I understood but the offering seemed a bit much given the threat heading our way. I assure you given my many years of church ministry, someone is always thinking about paying the bills the next week, so I get it.

Everyone left with hugs, well wishes and concern for fellow church members. As we returned home, I started packing our SUV with only the most critical items we required and prepared the family to leave the home. While the fire departments would usually share evacuation orders, I did not want to be stranded in the area while everyone else was attempting to exit the area. I looked at the far ridge across the valley where we lived high above the canyon below. I decided if we saw fire cross the ridge, I would load the family and head east for safety. Sure enough it happened and I loaded the family and moved further east to escape the fire's path. It was a good thing we left early because I needed more fuel to make the trip. With God's help, I got to the gas station before the area lost power. God was definitely watching over us at that moment. As we pulled out of our driveway, we prayed for our safety and thanked God for the home we had and asked Him to watch over it as we departed.

We headed east until we got to a small town where some friends from our church lived. We checked with them to inquire of their plans. They felt safe as the fire was still 20 miles away from them. They also offered shelter to my family. This was such a blessing as our daughters were close friends. They were able to encourage each other during the experience. I tried to work the next Monday from my SUV as most areas had lost power. Fortunately, I had a power adapter in the vehicle I could use to charge phones and computers. It was not only a good way to keep busy but people outside our area were able to share reports about the firestorm and advise us how to proceed. As my team in Los Angeles monitored the firestorm, they told me to consider moving west before the fire reached the town where we were in Pine Valley. With efforts to reassess the situation and noticing the smoke was definitely moving closer to us, we discussed plans with our friends. We all decided to move west toward Alpine as the firestorm had already devastated anything that could burn so it was unlikely to double back on its path eastward. There was no power in the area but it seemed safer given the fire was unlikely to return.

That afternoon we all took off in our vehicles and headed west. We had heard so many different stories about the fire, we were uncertain whether our home was still there or even if the church was still standing. As we entered Alpine, we could see so much destruction from the fire. However, the primary part of the town had been saved from the fire and many homes were still standing. To our rejoicing, we arrived at our home to find the ground covered in ash but everything on our property had been spared from the fire. We were so thankful to be home. Barb immediately offered sanctuary to many of our friends who did not have a safe place to be on this day. We did not have power, but we had a grill and a hand crank can opener which would sustain us for the days to come. I had just filled our garage freezer with beef from the butcher. The meat was going to be a loss so everyone at our house had steak for several days. We were eating good while it lasted.

The next day we made our way to the church. I had heard it also survived the firestorm. Again, we were thankful. While the fire had approached within a quarter mile of our home, the fire had surrounded our church. Looking at the church and surrounding area, it looked like a moon scape as everything was black and scorched except for this green oasis which was our church property. By this time the Santa Anna winds had calmed down and the brave firefighters were getting control of the fire lines. Devastation was everywhere we looked. People were digging around in ashes, which was once their homes, to find anything they could salvage. But there was our church. The chain-link fence we had installed surrounding our property was not a fire barrier. I don't even know how to describe this miracle. As we walked the property, not one single blade of grass had burned or even withered from the surrounding heat. On the outside of the fence, it was charred and black. On the inside of the fence, it was a beautiful green oasis which drew people from the community to come for shelter and assistance. President G.W. Bush and Governor Schwarzenegger has contacted our church to request permission to land the presidential helicopter in our parking lot so our leaders could tour the surrounding area and coordinate assistance. Even they were amazed at how God had protected this thirteen-acre parcel. How could one not see what God had done amid this devastation but to provide a sanctuary of ministry to those living in our community.

That evening Barb and I started to reflect on all the blessings we had experienced throughout this firestorm. We also reflected on the immense needs surrounding us. Fortunately, none of our friends had lost any of their property. But many of our neighbors were not as fortunate. I couldn't get over the image of people hovering in ashes looking for anything to restore happiness in their lives. They looked completely lost amongst their once treasured possessions. The next morning, I woke with new purpose in my heart as God spoke and told me to do something for our neighbors who were struggling. I got into my car with my family, and we drove to the closest grocery store with power. I bought bread, peanut butter, jam, cookies, chips and water along with brown paper bags. I had purchased enough supplies to make just over two hundred brown bag lunches which could be distributed to our neighbors. As we returned to the church to use a multipurpose room setting up tables for bag preparation, we became overwhelmed with the size of the project we had undertaken. After working for about an hour, we had completed just a few meal bags. We kept thinking about all those people who would need something to eat and drink that day while they wandered about their properties. The scale of the project we had undertaken was clearly more than my family could accomplish. Even if we could assemble these meals, how would we get them to all these families?

As always, God never starts a project without the means and commitment to finish it. The youth of our church started showing up. We didn't put a call out to them. They just started showing up asking if they could help. Before long there were thirty or forty older teenagers there helping with the assembly of the brown bags. In fact, Barb and I stopped preparing meals and started coordinating the resources God had sent for this project. Work moved quickly as the noon hour approached. All the bags were ready. We gave ten bags to each driver and a couple of assistants to ride along to hand out meals. Each driver was given an area to cover. They were to do nothing more than approach burned out homes with people wandering around and offer them a brown bag, a prayer, and a card with information about how to reach our church for more assistance.

The next Sunday our church was filled to overflowing with people from all over the community who had come to not only witness the miraculous oasis, but to worship a Savior who had been so kind to them and considered their needs amidst all the loss they had experienced. God was in our midst receiving all the glory for the work he had done amid the devastation of the fire.

I never got comfortable with those evil winds as long as we lived in Alpine. I even had to flee a couple more times for safety as the fires were nearing our town again. Fortunately, we never experienced another firestorm in our community like this one. I will never forget that firestorm nor the presence of our God who directed our decisions and our ministry those days. So many times, we blame God for the things that happen to us. We forget this world is full of trouble. As a sinful people inhabiting this planet, we cause most of the trouble. The presence of God in the midst of trouble is its own oasis. God offers help to those who seek Him and peace to those who love Him. He also knows how-to put-up fences so that old devil can't seek and destroy what belongs to God. Not even a blade of grass should God not allow it.

Chapter Twelve: Hugs on the Mountain Top

The Lord appeared to us in the past, saying: "I have loved you with an everlasting love; I have drawn you with unfailing kindness." Jerimiah 31:3

From time to time the men in our church would take what we called a men's retreat and head to Big Bear for a mountain top experience together. About thirty men from ACF would meet at the church and drive up Big Bear Mountain just west of Los Angles to the beautiful little town of Big Bear. Typically, we joined other men from other churches at a retreat center. The men stayed in bunk houses and cabins. We would have good food, fun activities and gather in the evening for a worship time together.

One year, I remember staying in the bunk house. The extended weekend provided great times for our guys to connect with each other. However, this particular evening, my buddy John decided to join us in the bunk house. After lots of storytelling and joking around, the men started to settle down for sleep. Then it quietly started. The men would start to snore. It started softly and then it grew a little more. Kind of like Whoville but not quite as cute. It was almost tolerable until my friend John dozed off to sleep. In all my years, I had never heard snoring like this before. It was so loud the windows would literally rattle as he exhaled. I laid there all night long begging God for quiet so I could also get some sleep. About that time the furnace would start up and all the men including John would quite down with the surrounding noise. Then like a wicked scheme and just before I could get to deep REM sleep, the furnace would shut off and the cycle would start again. Each and every night this would occur. At our last dinner gathering before we returned home, I choose to give my friend a new name. From that day on we called him Chainsaw. When I met his wife the following week at church, I blessed her and told her there had to be a special crown in heaven for sharing a bedroom with Chainsaw all those years. I took mercy on her and said I would pray for her regularly. Clearly, this recognition of sleep abnormalities opened a floodgate of agony she needed to share about her painful life experience. All I can say is the next year, we all made sure Chainsaw had his own cabin so the rest of us could get some sleep.

Other times we might choose to rent a large cabin on Lake Arrowhead. This was also fun as we got to be just our guys and do things the way we wanted to do things. As we were not expected to be on our best behavior among other groups of men, it was usually full of fun times and many pranks. On one occasion I remember getting all the men's attention as I attempted to demonstrate my care for world conservation. I was laughing so hard that I could barely get the joke out. Looking back, I struggle to understand why my buddies didn't think it was that funny. To this day I still laugh about my antics. I had two bottles of Arrowhead bottled water that I felt needed to be returned to the wild. So, I asked the men to join me by the lake. I then opened the bottles and released them into the lake exclaiming, "Be Free...Return home to the freedom of the wild". Following my side show and with the support of several of the men present, I managed to drop butt first into the cold glacier water. Good thing we had a fire going so I could burn some carbon to dry out and get warm. I have decided that I might not be the best advocate of conservation. In the future, I will just keep all such demonstrations to myself. Unfortunately, some people just can't appreciate my advanced life view.

Now it's time to tell the story for which I chose to write this chapter about. This story has also been in my heart and what happened there changed my relationship with Jesus forever. We were at the retreat center again. All the men were gathered in the worship center for evening worship. It was an amazing evening. Hearing a few hundred men praise God in song is almost Pentecostal. This night in particular, I could feel God's Spirit amongst the men worshiping. The worship leader led the men in my favorite song at the time, "Hear Our Praises". Even now I catch myself singing the chorus of this song, "From the mountains to the valleys, hear our praises rise to you. From the heavens to the nations, hear our singing fill the air." Maybe it was the location being on the mountain having just driven up from the LA basin where I could visualize the sound of praise filling the earth around us. It was a special time. The men kept wanting to sing the song, so the worship leader kept repeating the song for us until we were all sung out. At that time a local pastor took the stage and opened his bible and asked a question. "What do you have that God wants? Are you willing to give it up for Him?" He spoke to us for almost an hour, but it seemed like minutes as he began to wrap up his message. As he closed, he challenged the men again with the question. What do we have that comes between us and God? Are we willing to go to God and ask Him what we need to get out of our lives to so we can have a fulfilled relationship with our heavenly father. Rather than completing the closing songs and prayer, the minister dismissed all the men with instructions to go out into the surrounding area on the mountain and find a place to be alone with God. Use this time to put yourself before God and ask Jesus what he wanted from you.

I left the worship center and found a place alone just a short walk away where I could be quiet and pray. It was a wooded area surrounded by brush and large pine trees. In the midst of this small grove was a clearing just my size. As I had been making my way to this place, I was already anticipating the things God would want from me. I had two possessions on my mind. One was my baby grand piano, and the other was my motorcycle. These two things kept going around in my mind as things that might rise to the level of conflict with my relationship with God. I really didn't think they were that important. But then again, I had never really asked God if there was anything he wanted from me. I was already working though the struggle in my heart as to my willingness to surrender whatever God asked of me. This was an anxious time for a few reasons. First, I had hoped I had not put anything in my life of which I loved more than Jesus. Then, if I had done such a thing, I wanted to be sure I could repent and set my heart right with God. Of course, I also considered what my life would be like without my music and without those treasured bike rides with Barbie. I just had to trust God and surrender all.

I paused in the opening of that grove and reached to the heavens as I sought God in my prayers. I then summoned the courage to ask God what I had that he wanted. For a moment, there was silence in my soul as I listened for God's voice. Then I heard from God. He said so clearly this statement to me. "I want you to tell me how much you love me." I was broken. My heart sank within me thinking I had not taken the time to express my love for Jesus. While I was so busy in life serving my church and serving my family, I had failed to nurture the most important relationship in my life. As I composed myself from the sword that is able to pierce both heart and soul, I cried out to Jesus over and over, I love you. I am so sorry for not telling you how I feel about you. I vowed from that moment on, I would always remember to tell Jesus of my great love for him each time I prayed.

Then something happened to me. I felt something grab me. I mean physically grabbed me around the chest and back and was squeezing the air out of my lungs. I couldn't breathe. At first, I thought I had encountered a brown bear who had snuck up on me. But I looked and I was all alone. I realized Jesus was holding me in His arms and pulling me close to Himself. At that moment, I felt all the love that Jesus had for me. It was absolutely overwhelming. I don't even have words to describe the experience but to say for the first time I had experienced Jesus' love without bounds.

I tried to share the experience with some of the men, but they just couldn't connect to what I was trying to say. Maybe they were shocked I had never experienced anything like this before. But knowing these guys, I doubt they would miss an opportunity to share such an experience with me if they had the chance. When I got home, I couldn't wait to tell Barbie what had happened on the mountain. She was blessed and we grew together once more. As we prayed together from that moment on, I also made certain to tell Jesus how much I loved Him. I don't say these words because they are beautiful to speak or to gain recognition from others. I say these words because Jesus loves me. And because I remember that time together in the woods when His presence literally took my breath away.

Chapter Thirteen: The Experience Bank

Now, I want to focus a bit on life lessons. For all the times in my life when I have been blessed to witness the presence of God, I treasure the experience and seek to apply something useful to my life and the way I live. I call this The Experience Bank. I want to take you to Romans 5:1-5.

> *Therefore, since we have been justified through faith, we have peace with God through our Lord Jesus Christ, through whom we have gained access by faith into this grace in which we now stand. And we boast in the hope of the glory of God. Not only so, but we also glory in our sufferings, because we know that suffering produces perseverance; perseverance, character; and character, hope. And hope does not put us to shame, because God's love has been poured out into our hearts through the Holy Spirit, who has been given to us.*

In this scripture, we see a cycle of spiritual living. When I discovered this teaching, it helped me strengthen my outlook when troubles come my way. The Bible teaches us this world is full of troubles. I especially connect to Revelations when Jesus refers to this life as "The Great Ordeal". How we face each day of our life matters in how we face tomorrow. Picture in your mind yourself standing amid the ordeal called your life. As you stand there recognize that God intends for us to have peace. Peace only comes from Jesus and by faith in His promises for us. Also know that peace is not a state of being but a process we work out in our lives. When we seek peace, we actually have to make the peace so it can exist with us. When two countries seek peace with each other, they have to work out that agreement and then commit to maintain it, so the peace continues. God expects us to maintain the peace he offers us through the way we live our lives and how we respond to this life in being faithful to God as well as obedient to His ordinances.

Next, consider a large circular cycle surrounding your peace. This cycle starts with Faith also called hope. Hebrews says, "*Now faith is confidence in what we hope for and assurance about what we do not see*". We even put our faith in the hope of peace which God has promised us. We have absolute confidence God will give us peace although we have no way other than faith to believe it to be possible. But faith untested is not real faith. Let me assure you it is not God's faithfulness that we need to test but rather the certainty of faith in our own hearts and minds that our hope in God will sustain all. You can't get closer to understanding God Almighty without knowing His commitment to your peace. Let's be practical for a moment. We say we follow Jesus because we love Him and want to spend eternity with Him. Imagine if you had not struggled in this life, where would that faith be in your last moments to give you confidence that your eternal peace is awaiting you. When you know with confidence, it absolutely changes everything you do in this life. Faith in God is nothing more than believing God is Almighty and has and will do everything He has spoken. You have to experience this faith before you can grow in the peace that passes all understanding which can rule in your life today. I love that thought. I need that peace to sustain this ordeal called life. So, to do that, I need to follow this scripture so I can rest in my faith for I need to know my God is always faithful. So how do we do that?

I must face my sufferings in this life. There is no escaping this reality. I used to have a pastor who believed if you're not in a trial, its either because you just finished one or you're just starting another. I am not sure it is quite that persistent, but I do know trials come and when they come, they are real. As I look back over my life, I come to recognize many of the sufferings or trials I experienced in my life were preparing me for things to come. I started to realize I gained strength from having survived trials, which would strengthen me to survive the one I was in. As a younger man, I felt great trepidation about the struggles I faced. I would cry out to God to find me and save me from this experience. Begging to have this just go away was sometimes my greatest prayer. Honestly, looking back, some of those struggles were not even worth the furrow of my brow. Compared to the God whose faithfulness sustained me day to day, I really had yet to face anything of substance. None-the-less, these struggles and trials had to come so I could experience the peace God was working out in my life. Let's be honest with each other, when there is a trail in our life, we are more apt to turn to God for help. God absolutely knows how we were created and how we operate. Stir the pot of our comfort and happiness a bit, and let the tempest run amuck, and we eventually get to our knees in prayer. This eventuality is really the next part of this growing in peace. How can struggles make a meaningful difference in how we live day to day.

Struggles forces perseverance. Character is the substance of who we are. Perseverance is another word for patience. Patience is probably the least appreciated spiritual attribute of life for any Christian. The old adage where the man prays for patience and asks God to give it to him right now is about how we approach this part of our trials. As the trial continues, we just want it to stop. We ask for what we do not understand. Rather than begging for an escape, we continue the trust in God and follow His teachings while this trial continues in our lives. The purpose for this trial is usually greater than just what is happening to us. As God's children we are part of a greater family. As we share our needs with other believers and ask them to also pray to God, what we are really asking God to do is help us with our patience while He completes the good work, He has started in us. We need to take the focus off ourselves and consider how God can impact many lives with the struggle we are facing. How wonderful is it to hear a fellow believer has been healed by God after you have prayed for that healing. Don't you know God always heals? We don't always like the way the healing comes but when we bear witness, the healing is a blessing to everyone who put their hope in God. Have you ever prayed for someone to find a job so they could better provide for their family. How blessed were you when you realized this person had been provided the job God absolutely wanted that person to have and in doing God provided not only for the basic needs but the fulfillment of that person's purpose in life. The patience we seek it to believe with hope that God is doing a work in our life, and we should hope in doing God brings glory and honor unto himself as the Almighty who loves and cares for his own. Don't be in such a hurry to find relief as the journey will do the very things you need rather than finding that easy escape. What could be more important than finding the escape.

Perseverance builds character. People who know me, think I'm quite the character already. I suspect they question the quality of the perseverance I have experienced in my life as I can be a cut-up and have a twisted sense of humor. But those who know me well also know how much love is in my heart and how much I trust my Heavenly Father for everything. The person you become as you complete the experience of the struggle is how you see yourself and how others see you. I used to think if I failed in the patience of my trial or failed to trust in God through the process, I would be a failed believer. That is not even close to what God sees as the outcome for the process. Sometimes when the trial is over you look back and realize God was there all along trying to help you through the struggle. Character is all about building off the post-trial assessment and putting that learning into your Experience Bank. This is all more than just the measure of the man. This is how you work out you peace with God. When you start to realize how faithful God is, you will not be so easily shaken when the next struggle comes your way. You can grow into that tree that is planted on solid soil and doesn't blow over as it did when it was planted in the sand. Your character is your life with its foundation rooted in the peace of Jesus. What do you see when you look inside your life. Do you live with fear that the next straw will break the camel's back, or do you believe with real hope that your God is able?

When this scripture first spoke to me, I was teaching children in our children's church at ACF. I referred to this process as building our Experience Bank. Just like they could go to their piggy bank and get a dollar that they had put away for a future need, we should also draw on the learnings from our sufferings in this bank so we can be confident of God's continued peace when the next trial starts. What a perfect type of transaction for life. When we face a trial, start looking for the amazing thing God is going to do for you and others in your life. I assure you it is coming. Then when you have reached the other side of that trial, take measure of the experience, and hide it in your heart so that when you need a withdrawal, there is a treasure there to sustain the hard times. God expects all of us to grow in our walk with Him. We are not to nurse on milk all our days but sustain ourselves in the meat of His salvation. When this happens to you the greatest thing you could ever want will occur. The love of God will be poured into your life in abundance. When you fully recognize just how much God loves you and will watch over you all the days of your life, the peace in your soul is full. Your hope is complete. You will journey the rest of your days in confidence knowing Jesus holds you in His hands.

Again, I have nothing to boast about the character of the man who I have become. It was God who gave me the hope. It was God who formed my character from the trials he led me through. It was His presence in my life with overwhelming love that made me what I am. And what am I? Just a poor sinner God made with a choice to be made as to how I would seek hope in this life. I am still a work in process and far from the completed good work God has started in me. How do I know? Because when He is finished preparing me in this life, He will invite me to be home with Him for eternity. It's all about God's presence in my life. I can't make it better on my own. But God can strengthen me when times are tough, so I remember I matter to the Almighty Father.

Chapter Fourteen: A Purpose Driven Savior

People have told me I should be careful suggesting I know God's purpose. Let me be clear, I don't mean to overreach in this chapter, but I do wish to lay out an understanding I have reached as I have gotten to know my Jesus. It's such a beautiful story that it must be told. So please reserve your judgement about this title until you get to the end. Then you can come and tell me what a nut I really am. That will be ok because I assure you many people have already beat you to it. I am still compelled to share what God has taught me about His grand design for humanity. Despite what people say to me, I am human, and I belong to this humanity God created. While you may disagree with this statement, let me assure you that many doctors and scholars have confirmed I am indeed human. As such I was created by God. And as such, I had to search for the why about this life. Why am I here. Why did God create me or any other human for that reason. Why does eternity matter in this life we live today. The big one everyone asks, why does God allow sufferings in our lives. I had so many questions. While the Bible is full of information about these questions, yet it does not simply spell it out and connect the dots with a nice Q&A reference document. This understanding comes from reading God's word and getting to know His heart.

I'm going to skip the first question of relevance because that was the easiest for me to accept. Did God create? Being somewhat educated in the sciences and having had personal experiences with God, I really had no need to question this any further. As there is God our Father, then this is His creation and His Son, Jesus, rules over heaven and earth and His Spirit lives within the lives of His children. Thus, the Bible must come from God's teaching and inspiration and thus the Bible can be relied upon to guide me towards answering the other questions I had about mankind and why. As a living testament and a student of the Bible, I have confirmed in many times and many ways, it is the Word of God. I would ask anyone who believes otherwise to prove to me that God did not create everything and prove it with a conviction of spirit that comes from their belief in creation. I don't think that can be done.

So, let's start with the most foretelling scripture in the Bible. *"God saved us and called us to a holy calling, not because of our works but because of his own purpose and grace, which he gave us in Christ Jesus **before the ages began**, and which now has been manifested through the appearing of our Savior Christ Jesus, . . ."* (2 Tim 1:8-10). How amazing is this. God had a purpose for His creation and each and every one of us were created and called to God before the Heavens and Earth were ever even formed. The only event yet to occur was our arrival on this planet at a time ordained by God for your specific existence. This idea of purpose suggests a plan was formed by God before anything was created on this earth. Part of that plan included our own path to salvation. *The lamb of God "was foreknown before the foundation of the world but was made manifest in the last times for your sake." (1 Pet 1:20).* Even the idea that Jesus would die on a cross for our sins was planned before the first human received the breath of life from a Holy God.

If you feel this span of humanity was scripted like a dramatic intrigue, you would be correct. Why would God do this. Again, we can see in the scripture it was all about love. As a child many of us learned John 3:16, For God so Loved the world... Never lose your bearings in this life because it is imperative no matter what is going on around you, the purpose behind everything about humanity is God's love. For some reason, God chose to love us and He desires to be loved by us. Honestly, I would have thought the love of His angels would be better than a sinner like me. That was not the love God sought. Remember that God gave us a Holy Calling. What is a Holy Calling? It's simply a free will of choice. Choice by faith is what this love is built upon.

Before humans ever reached our point of creation, God had already created heaven where he lived within the Holy Trinity of God with his angels and the other amazing creatures described in the Bible about heaven. God created angels to love Him. I am often amazed when I think about the Seraphim Angels in heaven. These angels love God so much they seek to be in His presence. They surround the throne of God speaking praises for all eternity. This sounds delightful. Why wouldn't God be satisfied with the legions of angels who surround Him in Heaven. What is so different about humans and angels that God purposed a plan to include both beings? It's all about choice, faith, and free will. Angels were created to love God. They needed no faith to love God as they were created in His presence. Actually, the only choice of will an Angel could make would be NOT to love God. We all know the story of the mighty Arch Angel Lucifer. He made that choice and as a result was cast out of God's presence to roam the earth and become a tempter to the coming humanity. There can be no redemption for a fallen angel as the bible makes it clear, *(Romans 10:9) if you confess with your mouth that Jesus is Lord and believe in your heart that God raised him from the dead, you will be saved.* You must believe which means at one point you did not believe. Clearly all the angels in heaven believe there is a God who died for our sins. There is no redemption without faith in God's plan for our salvation. As an angel cannot live by faith, there can be no redemption.

Let's think of this another way in terms we can better appreciate. Think about the love of your family. Why do they love you? Clearly, we can find many examples in this life where children despise their parents or marriages fall apart because they do not love each other. When you think about someone who loves you, you get this wonderful feeling inside because you know they choose to love you. I remember the day of my marriage when Barbie stood before everyone we knew and declared and pledged her love to me. This was her choice to make of her own free will. It is because of that kind of love; I feel loved and covet being loved that way. We are made in the image of God who also loves being loved that way. The great purpose God set out to create was by giving humans a choice to love Him.

So why does there have to be so much suffering in this life. Why can't it be just one big loving experience. First, I encourage you to remember a few things from God's perspective. This time on earth is primarily for preparation for eternity. It is to prepare each of us to make a choice about Jesus and then hopefully encourage others to find that same love and make that same choice. Second, this existence is only a small fraction of our entire existence as a human. Our time on this little blue dot inside this vast universe is as insignificant to eternity as earth itself is within the universe. This short existence is just the beginning of our relationship with God. He was so excited to create you in His image just to give you an opportunity to choose. But we all know that as human beings we prefer to wonder and find instant gratification. That is why there are sufferings. Would you ever want to leave the garden of Eden? Of course not. It was perfect. Nothing hurt, ached or was broken in life. But as we do not seem to stay focused on God's purpose for us, sin entered and separation from God became the default for mankind. The only way to close that gap would be to choose Jesus in faith for our eternal love. When everything is going good in your life, you tend to focus on yourself and your happiness. But bring a bit of trial and it is not too long before you're on your knees crying out to God for help. Some people think this is cruel for God to allow such sufferings. But without sufferings, people are not broken to seek God. It is our nature to wonder. God promises to fix all of our brokenness when He redeems us into eternity. Is it really cruel to struggle in this life, knowing that this struggle is designed to open your hearts and recognize your need for something better that only God can offer? God makes it clear He does not want any to perish but for all to have eternal life with Him. In Revelations 21 God speaks and assures us that this suffering will be the first things to go when we reach our time in eternity. The old order of things will be gone away. It does not please God to see our struggles but remember Jesus himself choose to share in our struggles so we could have hope knowing these same struggles are known by the Father and are not eternal.

Could there have been another way to create beings with a free will to choose to love God without struggles? I don't think so. If we were created like the angels, we would arrive in heaven and once again choose to revolt against God. We would never understand the sense of living in separation from God. I know the pain and sufferings of this life, search within me to find my savior. I also know having experienced living amongst suffering and separation from God, I would never choose to live without Him. Heavenly eternity is guaranteed to be a place full of those who share in the love of God. Each person there will be there because they chose to love God and put their trust in His plan.

I guess anyone could suggest they would have done it differently had they been God. They think they would have spared everyone from heartache and suffering. I guess anyone could suggest God is cruel and unloving because of this suffering and say they could never love a God who would allow such things as war and famine to occur. I guess those same people would believe they know better than God just a Lucifer did and that is why there is no place in heaven for them. I could also suggest that if any of you are as Almighty as God to design a more perfect plan of redemption and love, then please feel free to begin your own creation of the universe or be still and contemplate the right of the Almighty Creator to have his plan to complete a perfect work in your life. A work He loves and cherishes so much that He would create everything He created just to get an opportunity to share eternity with you. That love drives me and compels me to love God with all my heart.

God also understands if you find it difficult to accept his plan as the perfect plan for your life. Look at Job. I doubt many of us has suffered more than Job. Even Job cried out at God because of his sufferings. God understood and still loved Job. Even Job questioned why God had to allow such suffering in his life. Job got to a point in his life where he couldn't understand the why or how about his own personal losses and sufferings. Then God spoke to Job and suggested he stop questioning the one who was able to speak the entire universe into existence and simply trust. As hindsight is so clear now, the story of Job is a beautiful story for believers to rely upon today to strengthen our trust during troubled times. We can be assured God is watching over us. He will direct blessings to come and replace the pain of suffering. Ultimately, Job put his entire trust in his Creator and submitted to the greater work God was doing in his life. What trust Job had achieved through such struggle and doubt. God never gave up on Job even when Job gave up on God. The journey, while difficult to consider, had blessings not just to Job but also for his future family and all those who would read his story.

If I have a favorite passage of scripture in the whole Bible it is *Revelation 21:3; And I heard a loud voice from the throne saying, "Look! God's dwelling place is now among the people, and he will dwell with them. They will be his people and God himself will be with them and be their God."* What an anticipated announcement to start eternity. It's almost like all of heaven including God Almighty is awaiting anxiously the time when this can occur. How can anyone read this understanding all that God has done to fulfill his purpose to demonstrate how much he wants to be with us.

It was important for me to have come to this understanding as a younger man because the years and the struggles yet to come in my life would be more than I could have borne had I not known the greater purpose God had for all of us. It all mattered to God, and I knew no matter the struggle, God was there and able to provide comfort and assurance to me every day no matter what that day had for me.

Chapter Fifteen: Jesus Always Heals Completely

For we walk by faith, not by sight. We are confident, then, and would prefer to be away from the body and at home with the Lord. So, we aspire to please Him, whether we are here in this body or away from it. 2 Corinthians 5: 7-9

God had been preparing me for this next part of my life. Even to be sure I had the right pastor at this time of my life. I used to listen to my pastor pray for the sick and the families who had lost loved ones. He used to say, Jesus always heals, and Jesus always heals completely. It didn't ring true to me at first but as time passed by, I began to truly appreciate the truth of this promise from God.

The first person I loved and lost in my life was my Granny. As a newlywed and a new father, I got word one morning my Granny had passed from her battle with cancer and had gone to be with Jesus. I was fortunate to have been able to make a trip back to visit her before she turned worse. She had the opportunity to meet Barbie and we shared a precious time together. It was hard to leave because I was fairly certain that would be the last time, I would see her on this side of eternity. When my mom called with news of her passing, I was sad but relieved. I was relieved to know her suffering was over. I understood her struggles with cancer to be very difficult and I didn't want her to hurt anymore. I trusted God had redeemed her with a heavenly body and she would never know pain again. Yet while we were all still here, our hearts ached because we missed her loving hugs and kisses each and every time we got to see her. I wouldn't be able to call her every week and visit like we had done for many years. I didn't have the money to make a trip back for the funeral. I had decided to make the trip before she passed. I am glad I did because those are the memories I wanted to have. It has been many years now since her passing, but God is still healing those left behind including me. I did feel great peace when my Granny passed as I knew she was in the arms of Jesus giving him all my hugs and kisses for now at least.

Later my father-in-law passed unexpectedly. This was a very difficult time for our family and especially my wife. But then again, as we got some time to reflect on things, we were blessed to have had a call with him just a couple of days before he passed. My father-in-law was very much an introvert and had little to say. He had feelings but kept them to himself. It was rare to get much more from him than some silly humor that was old and cold. I loved it. He grew up in Maine and like many from that area had a very stoic way about himself. But to get to talk to him just before he passed and have him express how much he loved us; was a treasure we could not have valued more. Charlie had struggled with his health for many years. While we missed him, again, we knew his struggles with health were over and Jesus was so excited to have him home. This hope in the promise of our reunion continues to be the healing we need as we remember his place in our lives.

My father was a special man in many ways. He started out as a print shop manager for the local newspaper. He was a rising star in our little town of Paris Tennessee. He was the president of the Jaycees. This was a men's group who seemed to do good things in and for the community. He was likely to become a partner in the print shop and we had a new home he had just built. Things were on the right path for our family when the calling came. I was eight years old when I saw my father leave his seat at the church and walk towards our pastor. God had called him to be a pastor. Change was coming in our lives to an extent we could have never really understood.

One of my father's former pastors was having serious health issues. This all started just after my father accepted the calling to the ministry. One day news came out that Dr. Ellis was in the hospital and not expected to live. Later that day, Dr. Ellis was pronounced dead at the hospital as his heart had stopped beating as he had succumbed to his sickness. After a few minutes, Dr. Ellis awoke, and his sickness was completely gone. Everyone was in amazement as this was a miracle which no one could seem to explain. Several weeks went by and even as a young boy I remember the day when Dr. Ellis and his wife came by our home to visit with us. Dr. Ellis started to share a story with my father about his passing. The story was beyond amazing as he described what happened in those minutes before he awoke at the hospital. It seems Dr. Ellis met Jesus in those minutes who told Dr. Ellis he would be returning to earth to live a while longer as Jesus needed Dr. Ellis to mentor my father's preparation for the ministry. Talk about having God's presence in your home. My father was speechless. Neither of them shared that story very much as this was something God had purposed of them. Dr. Ellis did help my father get his affairs in order and prepared to start attending a Bible college in a nearby town where he would eventually receive his bachelor's degree in divinity and begin his work as a full-time pastor.

I guess when your ministry starts with such a miraculous blessing, you can expect God to be with you throughout your years of service. That is exactly what God did for my father. He pastored a few churches. He was loved and appreciated for his leadership and devotion to loving and caring for God's people. Over the years my father had shared the gospel with many people and had the pleasure of baptizing thousands of people who had followed into the faith of the gospel. Beyond that he had served so many who were needing prayer and Godly counsel. My father also had a passion for his own family. He came from a large family and had eight siblings. As he entered the ministry, his heart for their own salvation was always top of mind. He would pray for them and share Jesus with each of them as often as he would see them. As the years passed, one by one, these siblings would come to know Jesus as their own savior. As they all got older, some of them started to pass. Both of my father's parents had passed as well as his two older sisters. My dad was the fourth child born into the family. The oldest brother was the one in the family who had made up his mind that he was never going to turn to Jesus. I didn't know this uncle very well but what I had known about him suggested a worldly kind of man who lived a simple and hard life. My dad never gave up praying and encouraging his brother to commit his life to Jesus.

My dad had retired and moved back to Tennessee. He was starting to have health problems of his own. When you grow up on a southern style meat and potatoes diet, it is not uncommon to have cardiovascular issues later in your life. My dad was no exception. If it could be fried, then it was going to be fried and served for dinner accompanied by an extra covering of salt. Breakfast was always our favorite meal. My dad expected a cooked breakfast each morning when I was a young boy living at home. I remember one morning as a very young boy when my dad had a real temper about himself, he lost control of that temper as he entered the kitchen and looked at what my mom had prepared for breakfast. There were fried eggs, bacon, sausage, and gravy all sitting on the table. One thing was missing as he looked over the table. He saw a bag of white bread on the table and no biscuits. In that moment my dad picked up a Melmac plate from the table and slammed it to the floor in anger. My mom and I were both shocked as this unbreakable plate shattered into many pieces. My mom, being so cool headed about the whole thing simply turned to the oven and removed the biscuits and sat them on the table. Without saying a word, my mom had reset the proper order of respect in her kitchen and my dad not only had a mess to clean up but also had to grovel to manage the apology. Clearly, my dad loved his southern food.

As my dad got into his forties, this all started to catch up with him. His blood pressure was a constant battle. The doctors tried to put him on a salt free diet and to cut out fried foods and sugar. This was a struggle for everyone in the family. Mom had to learn a new way of cooking. The food was still good and a bit healthier, but my dad wasn't satisfied. Let me give an example. One morning like many mornings my dad and I left to go fishing together. I met him at his house, and we pulled the boat to Puget Sound where we would launch and do some salmon fishing. It was a cold and damp morning. We had little success catching anything and finally decided to pack it in and go back home after the tide change had passed and we were still without any catch for the day. As we drove home, my dad started thinking about ice cream. He asked if I wanted to stop by the Baskin and Robins Ice Cream store and have a scoop of ice cream with him. Being the good son and not wanting to catch the wrath of my mother, I told my dad we should not stop as this was definitely not on his diet. My dad persisted and tried to convince me this one exception would not be a problem as he really missed having his peanut butter and chocolate ice cream. I resisted but he was persistent and suggested there was no need to inform mom about our little excursion. He even offered to treat me to an ice cream if I would just support his temptation to satisfy the craving. I eventually gave in, and we stopped for the treat. My dad assured me this was a rare exception, and he wouldn't do this again as it was also a rare opportunity to extend a visit with his son. As we entered the Baskin and Robins, the young man behind the counter extended a double scoop peanut butter and chocolate ice cream cone and welcomed Pastor Don back for his usual treat. The look on my dad's face as I turned to him as he had been caught in his cheat was priceless. I had never known my dad to outright lie to me before, but I guess when it came to his favorite ice cream, it was a price he was willing to pay. As we sat at the table to enjoy our treat, my dad started trying to apologize and explain the circumstances. I assured him no explanation was required as it was very evident what had been occurring on a very regular basis. Despite the begging and pleading, mom was going to hear about this, and my dad was going to have to work harder at controlling his diet.

As my dad turned fifty, he started needing more aggressive treatments for his cardiovascular issues. He was having vascular pains and the doctors were finding frequent plaque buildup in his arteries. It had almost become a routine procedure to have stents placed in his arteries to open the clogged blood vessels and restore them to health. I would speak to my dad at least once a week and I could hear in his voice his health was declining and his outlook on life was not as joyful as it had once been. My mom was busy caring for her father who was also ill battling congestive heart failure. This meant my dad spent time at home alone while my mom was attending to my grandfather. Growing old is not easy for so many reasons and fighting health issues keeps you from doing so many things you had hoped to do as you started retirement.

Having spoken to my father earlier in the week, he told me about his plans to visit his older brother who was very ill and dying before he traveled to Memphis for another stent procedure. During that visit with his brother my dad once again encouraged him to seek forgiveness and reconcile with Jesus accepting salvation for his soul. After my dad left without having assurance his brother would turn to Jesus, he went on to Memphis for his own medical procedure. As this was fairly routine, I had almost forgotten about the procedure. It was a Friday evening and as I had typically done, I went to the movies with my family. I left the phone off during the movie so we could enjoy some time together. After the movie I returned to our car and noticed I had messages from my mom. As I was driving and using the speaker on the car phone, my mom began to explain my dad had an aneurism on the brain during the procedure and bleed out on the table. The doctors could not save him, and he was on life support but had no brain activity. I had just lost my dad.

Somewhere between being broken over the news of losing my dad and trying to comfort my mom and my own family, I tried to hold it together to make plans to fly home for his memorial service and to be with my family as my mom had to make the transition to live as a widow. This was so hard to face, and I cried many tears in grief during those days. We struggled to get by together and then we got a call from my dad's family. Two days after my dad passed his older brother also passed. From the time my dad left his brother until the moments just before he passed away, he had been in a comma. His family had something to tell us about my uncle's passing. It seems just as he took his last breath, he rose up out of the bed and made a statement that stunned everyone. He said, "Don, what are you doing here?" My uncle had no way to know my dad had passed just a couple of days before. Clearly, my uncle had accepted the gospel and reconciled with Jesus that day when my father prayed one last time with his brother. During all this sadness, there was joy to be found. My uncle had reunited with my father in heaven as my father was waiting on the other side for his arrival. My father's greatest hope for his family had been fulfilled. He would spend eternity with his family.

I still miss my dad to this day. I used to call him all the time for advice and counsel about life. I didn't have google to give me tips on how to fix things like my son uses. I would spend hours on the phone with my dad trying to figure out how to fix a broken appliance or vehicle. He was a great help to me. Now I would have to find my way forward without his mentorship in my life. Kids now may not appreciate the value of learning from dads as they have the internet to solve their day-to-day challenges for how to do whatever. I also learned how to google whatever I needed but I really missed the bonding we would have together as my dad would share so much about his life experience with me during those conversations.

Knowing my dad is in the presence of God gives me great peace. I am not sure how my dad would have ever faced 9/11 or the societal changes and this new cancel culture. I know his heart would break over the indifference of God's purpose in people's lives today. I appreciate all my dad tried to do for our family. The greatest thing he gave me was an appreciation for who God is and what that can mean in my life. I try to share that same appreciation with my children and now my grandchildren. I know dad is waiting with Jesus for us on the other side of heaven with so many I have loved and lost before. It is Jesus who died and rose again and gave us victory over sin and death so we could have hope in the promise of life eternal with all those who love Jesus.

I realize this story is more about the presence of God in my father's life than my own. But having witnessed the presence of God in a man whom I loved deeply, has also impacted my own walk with God. It is important to share these experiences so we can encourage one another to seek that personal relationship with Jesus. It is the only power that always heals and heals completely.

Chapter Sixteen: It's Time to Go Home

Not forsaking our own assembling together, as is the habit of some, but encouraging one another; and all the more as you see the day drawing near. Hebrews 10:25

We were so happy at ACF, but it was time for a change. I knew it was time because the joy of serving with my brothers at the church had greatly diminished. While the church was growing, I was stuck. I was stuck because I could not bring myself to do something I knew the Lord wanted me to do. After months of struggling with this decision, I had to step down from church leadership and consider what would be next in our lives. I knew the church was needing changes in our pastoral leadership and I feared hurting a friend should I continue. I'm not sure if the issue was there to prepare us for a relocation or if I turned tail and ran from my responsibility. I have since sought forgiveness and reconciliation to those involved but this is always on my mind when I think about ACF. Regardless, there is one thing I am certain of, we needed to move back to Washington.

As we disengaged from ACF, we started the process of seeking a way to relocate. I had been thinking about it since our trip to Cannon Beach. During that trip I asked Barb if she ever wanted to move back to Washington. She was elated to hear the offer. I guess California never settled good with her as relationships were hard to maintain. The culture was somewhat superficial. She also missed her mom and her siblings. Not only did she want to move back but she wanted to do it quickly.

I started working with my company to discuss relocation. Since I worked remotely and most of my activities included air travel, I wanted to be sure I wasn't creating a new burden of cost for my business. I checked every flight from San Diego for comparable cost from Spokane. I really could not see any cost barriers and the travel time from my San Diego home to any place in Los Angeles was about a three plus hour commute. I learned I could fly to Los Angeles from Spokane in less than three hours. The other amazing thing was the travel from my home to the airport including parking and TSA checking was another two plus hours. I found my new home would be about thirty minutes from my desk to my gate. Clearly this was looking to be a good change for everyone. My company was completely supportive as long as I agreed not to leave the company. I was more worried the company might want to part with me given this relocation request. It turned out to be a boost in employment security which was a welcome outcome.

The decision to relocate occurred in 2007 which was just before the great recession. We were attempting to get everything ready to sell our San Diego home, but market prices were already under attack. Part of our goal was to clear enough from the Alpine home sale to purchase our new home mortgage free. In God's perfect timing we were able to sell the home in early 2008 and purchase our Cheney home. Everything was going great. We immediately started work on the home remodel. Both our kids decided to get married. Oh well, while we had this large home with lots of room for our kids, their hearts took them to marriage. Now we had a big empty house with an amazing extended family. Not a bad trade if you ask me.

According to all the popular thinking of the day, relocating with home sales, remodeling, weddings and empty nests were supposed to cause lots of stress and disfunction for us. Barb and I could not be more relaxed in our new home. Life was settling in very well except for one thing. We couldn't find another church. Honestly, after having served at ACF for fourteen years, I was tired. I felt like I needed a rest. Barb and I were also in our early fifties and recognized the need to deeply connect with a church family. We had friends at ACF but they seemed to come and go for various reasons. We wanted to put down real roots and become part of an enduring church fellowship. I didn't have the gumption for forcing change, but I wanted to serve others. I had hoped to reach retirement soon after moving to Cheney, but I also knew continuing to work was going to be in my near term future. We visited several churches in our community. We had established a 10-mile radius for finding our new church. We wanted to build on that sense of community rather than commute to a church further away. So, the search started. The first church we visited was a community church in Cheney. While on the surface this appeared appealing, something did not set right. We continued to search. Other churches we visited either had material issues with our beliefs, which were going to be divisive to a good fellowship, or they were just barely existing. We had noticed a sign about a church meeting in the local middle school close by. While we were not excited about the prospects of another church start up, we seemed to be left with no other options at the time. Given our options we finally decided to check it out.

The church was meeting in a school gym which was all too familiar to us. The pastor was the founder of the church and he had a passion to start this church to provide a contemporary church experience and evangelize the west plains of Spokane County. As I connected with the pastor, who would become a lifelong friend, Dave asked me to lead a newly organized elder board and help him launch the church organization. I knew better than to accept as that was not what my heart desired. I was somewhat of a church start up junky and couldn't resist the continuing calls to partner in this work.

There was so much work to do. We basically needed to create everything from a church mission statement to a constitution of bylaws for the non-profit organizational permits to establishing membership and operating roles. As with almost every church start up where we met in a school, they wanted a plan for us to leave. I never really understood that behavior as the school appreciated the money we paid them, but rules were rules. They could not agree to long term co-use of the facility with any other organization. This meant we had a short time to find another place to meet if this church was going to continue. Our men searched the community for possible locations to purchase. The church's treasury was not even strong enough to make an escrow payment. Options seemed very bleak. Then one of the board members commented on an empty church owned by the EVF association of churches. There was a sign on the door stating the church had closed down and a number for contact. Once I got the number, I gave them a call and asked about using their facility.

After visiting the small facility, it seemed like a good location for the church to meet. It was much further away from my home than I wanted but since I was in it, I pressed forward trying to find a way to secure the use of the facility. I met with the EVF leadership as they were eager to see this property put back to use in the Lord's kingdom. We had a great discussion about our church and what we were trying to accomplish in our community. The leaders were celebrating our journey and as the meeting concluded, they asked me what they could do to help. Once again, the Lord spoke to me with a crazy idea. This time and without hesitation, I immediately shared God's request with the EVF leadership. I told them we would like to use the church building. Then with all the boldness I could muster I requested the EVF association churches sign the title over to our congregation in exchange for a commitment to pursue the Lord's work using the facility. It definitely took these men by surprise. They asked if they could discuss the request with their peers then get back to me in a few days. Well, they did and then they called and asked when we could meet to sign over the title. What a blessing that was. The church members were amazed and excited to have this new facility which freed up monies used for rent that could be repurposed to other ministry work. We celebrated how only God could provide in such ways.

I continued to serve there but it wasn't long before I knew this was not where I was supposed to be. I had to leave, and God made certain of my departure. We had been in the community for four years and we were not any closer to finding the fellowship we sought. As we drove to church each week, we would pass by another church which was also outside our ten mile target. But we needed a place to go, and this seemed like a good alternative. As we attended this church, Barb got very sick. The time at this church was overshadowed by medical treatments and many hours of home isolation. We attempted to reach out to build connections at this new church which seemed to be promising. But when our need for any type of fellowship became emanate, only one dear widowed lady came along our side to comfort or encourage us. After another couple years of trying, we realized another failed attempt to connect with a church family and decided to cut our losses and move on again.

Barb and I knew what we needed at this point in our lives. We are approaching our sixties and clearly having experienced major health challenges isolated from other praying believers, we had to find the church God had always intended for us. Where would we find this church. We had been to every church in the community at least once and nothing seemed to match for us. Then one day we decided to go back to the community church in Cheney. I'll call this church CCC because that is what everyone else calls it. We walked into the church and to our surprise, our good friend Dave was sitting in the congregation with his lovely wife. We had not seen each other since I left his former church. None-the-less, the spirit between us rekindled like we had not lost any time together. Dave encouraged us to give CCC another chance. He mentioned the church had recently undergone some pastoral changes and was a true bible believing loving fellowship which would open up to us and make us part of their family. Dave was right. It wasn't long before we decided to commit to the church and started joining a small group along with other activities. We started to make lifelong friends like we had not experienced in many years. Our hearts were full as we looked forward to every opportunity to connect with this church. Even my daughter's family decided to visit with us. Before long, they started attending regularly and now are leaders in the church. What a blessing to share with my daughter. I get to see my grandchildren almost every Sunday for worship. My grandson and I like to go to men's breakfast together. Watching my family grow in the Lord is a wonderful blessing to experience. Both Tristen and Brooklyn came to accept Jesus as their savior and asked their old grandpa to baptize them. Talk about my full heart. But equally was the celebration from those within the church for our family. Friends became family and we continue to share in our blessings at CCC.

Unfortunately, after we joined CCC Barb had another health situation. This new health issue would result in yet another chronic care matter for us to face. This time our church came to our side and nurtured us with prayer and encouragement. It is difficult to be in a situation where we can't really contribute to the church's ministry and are on the receiving side of the equation. It can be humbling to be in this situation. Our CCC family has continued to reach out to us and prayed for us as we share this trial in our life with them. Good friends are hard to find. But finding Christian believers who are there to support you is one of the best experiences this life has to offer.

After leaving ACF, Barb and I had come to understand we had a great need in our hearts that only God could fill. We also had a journey to experience before we would find CCC. The warmness in our souls is something like eating a freshly baked cookie. The aroma of sweet fellowship filled our senses while their companionship filled our hearts. Experiencing God's presence with his people is the fulfillment of celebration in this life. I know with certainty should something ever happen to me; Barb would need a church family to support her. I know CCC would be there for her. We are also able to pray for others who also need fellowship and encouragement. The struggles of this world are real. God's presence is necessary to carry us forward. How beautiful are the vessels that carry God's light. I am truly blessed and pray that we are at CCC for the rest of our days, God willing.

Chapter Seventeen: Alright, Alright, Alright

I have told you these things, so that in me you may have peace. In this world you will have trouble. But take heart! I have overcome the world. John 16:33

It was a beautiful summer day in August 2008 as I returned home from a business trip. My mom was visiting, and I was looking forward to connecting with the family and enjoying our time together. But that was not to be. Earlier that day as Barbie was on the deck enjoying the sunshine with my mom and daughter when they both noticed something not quite right about Barbie. While she was feeling great and really enjoying her day, her eyes had an odd shade of yellow about them. As soon as I entered the house, this development was brought to my attention, at which time, I called our clinic to get an urgent appointment to assess the situation. After an examination, the doctor was concerned this was due to poor liver function and there seemed to be something showing on the x-ray that required further investigation. We were immediately sent for an MRI. The doctor asked us to stay at the MRI office until they read the results and she would call us and advise us on the condition. While we feared it could be so many things, we really didn't know what to expect but we knew whatever it was, our life was about to take a very serious turn.

That evening as we rested before going to in for the MRI, we prayed together asking God to help us face whatever was coming and to spare us from any suffering if it be his pleasure. Unfortunately, the MRI found a tumor blocking the area where the liver, gallbladder, pancreas, stomach, and intestine all came together. This mass was interfering with the liver function, and something had to be done quickly to allow the flow of digestive fluids past the blockage. The next task was to go in for an emergency endoscopy. I remember this day as being so long and difficult for Barbie. The clinic where they did this procedure was booked out for weeks. They decided to add Barbie to the end of the schedule that day which meant she could have nothing to eat or drink all day until after the procedure. The procedure didn't start until about 5 p.m. that day. I felt compelled to fast with Barbie and continue in prayer with our family. When the procedure was finally over, the doctor called me back to confirm he found a cancerous tumor and confirmed it must be surgically removed as soon as possible. He tried to encourage me as he assured me during the procedure, he had reviewed the tumor from every direction and while it was definitely cancerous, it was something that could be removed. He was optimistic about the survivability of the procedure. None-the-less, we had to get to a surgeon right away and plan for the operation.

We met our surgeon. He was a kind man and clearly understood the urgency of this situation and the concern we had for Barbie's wellbeing. He described the surgical procedure as a Whipple procedure. We learned it was the second most complex procedure done in the hospital, being second only to an esophageal replacement. The plan was to remove the tumor by disconnecting everything in the duodenum, which connected all those digestive parts to each other. He believed the surgery would go well as Barbie was otherwise healthy. The expectation was to be home in eleven days following the surgery. While that sounded challenging, we were a bit pleased as that meant Barbie would be home just in time for our 30th anniversary. Unfortunately, this plan would not go as well as expected. We were about to experience God in ways I pray no one has to experience. But this was to be our journey, God had us in his care. Each hour was a time to lean on God for support and assurance.

As Barbie left me that morning for surgery, many of our family and friends came to be with us. My daughter had a young son but wanted to be at the hospital with us. Fortunately, Barb's sister was so kind to offer to stay with him so Mandy could be with us. Our son and his family had moved back to San Diego to help with Adrelly's father who was also very ill. While they wanted to be with us, things were moving so fast, there was not time to get here in time. They stayed in close contact with me as this was heavy on their hearts as well. The surgery continued for several hours while my loved ones sat with me and encouraged me. I wasn't much for companionship but knowing they were there was very comforting. I was anxious about the outcome of the surgery despite the reassurances provided by the doctors. After almost ten hours of surgery, the surgeon came to me and shared an encouraging update assuring me he completed the procedure as planned and removed the tumor along with all the surrounding tissue providing excellent margins for recovery. Barb was on her way to a room at Deaconess Hospital on the 8th floor where she would be cared for during her recovery.

It was so wonderful to see Barbie ever though she laid there so helpless with so many devices connected to her. She was aware enough to recognize me and let me assure her all was well. She just needed to rest and recover. I had decided to stay with her as this was a big ordeal. I wanted to support her, and I really did not want her to be alone. I asked for a folding bed so I could sleep in the room with her. They offered to get one for me, but it didn't show up for two days. I spent those first two nights attending to her either in the armchair or would stretch out on the floor to rest just for a while. When that folding bed arrived, I was very glad to see it. Barbie had not really changed her condition much during the first few days. The pain medication kept her knocked out. As the days progressed, the doctors wanted her to have some light fluids and she was eager to eat popsicles when she could. It was weird because whatever she would eat would come right back up through a stomach pump. The goal was to provide fluids for hydration, but the real feeding came from a feeding tube in her belly. After four days of monitoring her recovery, the surgeon became concerned with her wellbeing. It appeared Barbie had contracted an infection. The doctors order a strong regimen of antibiotics. This included a pic-line added to her right arm to help facilitate the IVs for antibiotics. This treatment did not seem to be helping Barbie and her infection was growing worse rather than improving. On day seven, the surgeon decided he would need to go back into the operating room with Barbie in attempts to clean out the infection and replace the feeding tube which was now contaminated with the infection. Almost like starting over, Barbie was taken from me to the operating room. Many of our family were still with us as again they sat with me while she was away. It was so good to see her return and to hear the surgeon say he felt successful as had treated the infected areas directly with antibiotics. However, he wanted to continue the IV antibiotics for a few more days to make sure these stubborn bacteria did not make their way back.

Barb continued to rest, and I stayed by her bedside. I had so much time to pray for her recovery. I would cry out to God for some assurance. I would beg God for mercy and share my heart's desire to get Barbie back home. Home was another matter. While all this was going on, we were remodeling our house to expand our upstairs living room and add a craft room to the front of our house. Barb loved to spend her free time with her crafts creating all those things that only she could imagine. I made an effort with the construction crew to help me set up her craft room the day before she went to the hospital. I wanted her to have that experience there so it would make her want to fight to get better so she could come home and enjoy this space. The room had an 180 degree view of our property with somewhat of a hexagon shape about it. There was so much light in the room for her. Barb's mom and sisters came over the night before along with my mom and daughter who spent the evening before her departure in the craft room together. They shared time together and prayed together. It was an important time Barb needed to help prepare for the days ahead. I share this because I wanted Barbie to just come home and share our days together and enjoy this craft room which I had hoped to give her for our 30th anniversary. But that was not to be either.

About ten days into the hospital stay, Barb developed a blood clot in her arm. While serious, this is typically something easily resolved with blood thinners. The doctor ordered and administered a Heparin IV to help clear the blood clot. Pretty typical stuff but as I would come to know, nothing about this experience would ever be typical for Barbie. This beautiful woman had been the picture of good health all her life only having gone to the hospital twice for the birth of our children. We had no way of knowing she would be allergic to this medication. As I sat by her side that evening, her blood pressure started to drop. This is what was known as a Heparin Induced Trauma (HIT). The only way this could be reversed was to push saline into her as fast as they could to dilute the medication and clear it from her system. They hung bag after bag of saline as I watched her body start to swell from all the fluid. I tried to get some sleep that night as there wasn't anything more I could do but it was really difficult to sleep as I continued to watch her blood pressure drop dangerously low. She was non-responsive as the treatment persisted. But I did lay my head on my bed pillow and prayed my heart out as I felt I was losing the love of my life.

I had asked so many people to pray for Barb's recovery. I knew many people were praying but as I prayed, I receive nothing from God that would comfort me. I felt God was listening but I wanted to see Barb get better so I could bring her home. I wanted anything from God to have assurance and hope for our future together. During the days leading up to this moment, I had so many conversations with God about this entire situation. I felt very selfish asking God to give me what I wanted. God made it clear to me he also loved Barbie and created her for himself. He sought to spend eternity with her as this was always his perfect plan. I would plead to God explaining how hopeless my heart was that moment. I finally got to the point where I blamed God for this great hurt I was feeling. I told God that I couldn't help but feel this way. It was God who created Barbie so perfectly and made her to be my bride. She was the perfect loving companion for my life. While I appreciated God's point of view, this pain and anxiousness of losing the love of my life was more that I could bear. How could I not feel so desperate to lose the most amazing person God had made for just me?

As I laid there watching the blood pressure machine give less encouraging news, I rolled over on my side and again cried out to God. I knew no other thing to do at this time but ask my God to have mercy on me and let Barbie come back home with me cured from this scary cancer. In that moment, God spoke to me. I mean he spoke to me as clearly as any conversation I ever had. If this was a bible, I would write these next words in red type print as I know they came directly from Jesus. Here is what I heard him say, "Alright, Alright, Alright Already. Bill, I want you to know I have heard your prayers. I have heard the prayers of your children. I have heard the prayers of your family and friends from places all over this world. I want you to know, Barbie will be going home with you, and she will not die of this cancer." My heart was full of thankfulness and trust in that moment. I praised God with all that was within me for granting me this gift. To this day I do not understand why God did this for me as there are so many others who pray for God's healing mercy and still lose their loved ones into eternity. I did know, God was not finished with Barb's purpose here and this entire ordeal we were experiencing together was to have a greater purpose than I would understand in that moment. All of this was to bring glory to Jesus the Great Comforter and Healer of our Faith.

At that time, I turned to Barbie and tried to wake her up enough to tell her what Jesus had said to me. She held my hand as best she could. Gave me a squeeze and thanked me for telling her the news. I had so much hope in God's faithfulness I couldn't help but tell everyone what had happened. Most of them thought I had gone crazy from sleep deprivation, but I knew better. God's presence had come to me and comforted me in only the way Almighty God could do. Immediately, we started noticing improvement in Barb's blood pressure. She was coming back to us. While she put on over 90 pounds of weight that night from the fluids, she was awake the next morning. We did as much as we could to help resolve the fluid issues and after a couple of days, her weight dropped back down to a comfortable level. We were not done with the recovery process, but I never ever doubted again what the outcome of this journey would be.

We spent 39 days in the hospital before Barb was able to make the first trip home. I say first because there would be two more trips to the hospital before the ordeal was over. Chemotherapy was not easy as her body was weak from all the other treatments. There would be blood transfusions and various treatments to help her along the way. By the time we were finished with the hospital stays, we had logged 59 days at Deaconess Hospital in Spokane. While the people had been so good to us, we wanted nothing more than to move on from this experience and get on to the business of healing. Healing would take almost another year of treatments and regular imaging scans to monitor her recovery. After a year of struggle, we were starting to make real progress. Barb had experienced a dozen new medication reactions of various types. She had been diagnosed with about fifty different health issues during this time as well. Despite all that had come at us we continued. I recall one evening after an MRI imaging of her abdominal area, the Oncologist called with troubling news. They had identified something growing on Barb's liver. The Oncologist was a kind person who we got to know very well. This report from the radiologist troubled her more than it did me. I just reminded Barb of God's promise to not only send her home to me but also to resolve that cancer battle. My daughter challenged me after getting the news and wanted to know how it could be possible for God to make such a promise and now, we are facing a possible liver cancer diagnosis. I encouraged my daughter as well as all the others around us to have faith in God's plan including our Oncologist. After six long hours, we got another call back from our Oncologist. This time she was calling to share her day with us. She asked for several second opinions and gathered the tumor board together at the hospital to review the radiology report. After much evaluation, they had determined this was not a tumor but rather fatty tissue which had developed following the HIT event when the blood clot moved to the liver blocking the portal vein. The trauma from this event had caused the liver to struggle and this fatty tissue was now present. If you could have seen the look of assurance in my daughter's face as I took that call. All doubt was gone. As a family we were holding on to our faith and moving forward together now.

Another year or so later Barb and I got to the point where we could really open up and talk to each other about the entire ordeal. It was then Barb shared something with me she had experienced that evening when Jesus spoke to me. She had a vision of Jesus standing in our doorway. She described him as beautiful and calming and told her he was not coming for her now. As we put the events together, I began to realize at the exact same time Jesus was speaking to me, he was also giving comfort to Barbie. We were once again in amazement of God's perfect healing and mercy on our lives.

While all of this was going on, I could begin to understand what good could come of such trauma and pain. As Barb and I look back, I can tell you we would not trade this experience for anything. I assure you we do not want to live this experience again, but this ordeal brought us so much closer together. Our prayers together were full of meaning and purpose. We had compassion for others like we had never experienced before. God had changed us and grew us closer to himself and each other in ways I did not think possible.

I remind you again, I do not tell these stories to boast of God's favor on me or to suggest in any way I deserve favor from

God over anyone else. I do share it to be a testament of God's presence in my life. At a time when Barb needed healing, she was healed as was many in my family and I was healed beyond anything I could have imagined. We still give thanks for God's presence in our lives during those difficult days. I do know one thing for sure, whatever God puts before you, he is there. He will not leave you alone and despite what you think you need to carry on, He is the greatest love you will ever need.

Chapter Eighteen: A Loving Family

Children are a gift from the LORD; they are a reward from him. Children born to a young man are like arrows in a warrior's hands. How joyful is the man whose quiver is full of them! He will not be put to shame when he confronts his accusers at the city gates. Psalms 127: 3-5

I think back to when Barb and I started a family. It was an exciting time to meet our children. While the blessings were immeasurable, the work to raise children was hard. Let's be honest, every man remembers those sleepless nights and the rigors of raising a child. Then there is the financial cost, and the list goes on. I never imagined as those children turned to teens that their view of dad would also change. Sometimes it is more than one can bear but you just keep on loving them.

After our first child was born and had completed the excruciating experience of a 42-hour labor, I was certain Barb would not want any more children. I know for myself, having survived that experience without any medications and sleep deprivation, who would knowingly choose to do anything like that again? Within a few days of being home with our daughter, Barb was talking like nothing difficult had ever happened and looked forward to our next child. I thought she had amnesia. How could she have forgotten we had just been through? But it didn't matter at all. She had a loving mother's heart and especially loved babies. She would hold Mandy close and look at her for hours. The feeding, bathing, laundry and just trying to understand what the baby needed was also a big job. Again, did I mention the sleep deprivation? Still, we loved our daughter. We had her close with us in the bassinet next to our bed for the first few months at home. I remember when Barb and I discussed it being time to move Mandy into the baby bed in the adjacent room. My first reaction was immense happiness as I could feel a full night's sleep coming my way. When we moved her, I found it even more difficult to sleep as I lay awake all night just listening to her breathing to make sure she was alright. There is just no other way to say it, these kids just get you hooked all the way and there's no escaping...not that one would ever want to get away.

A couple years later Barb was ready for another child. Then came Nick. I thought this might be easier as I understood boy stuff and for some reason, I assumed infant boys would be easier to raise than infant girls. Boys would somehow be tougher and more resilient. That was not the case. In fact, when Nick arrived, he was immediately rushed to the NICU because of respiratory issues. Someone had just as well shot a cannon into me as I felt desperation in those moments. He was to be alright. Actually, he was more than alright. I remember visiting him under the heat lamps as he lay in that little plastic baby tray. He was a big baby. After watching him scream for a while and just turn all shades of red and blue, it was more than obvious any respiratory concerns had passed. We called him our deep-dish Nicky pie. I guess it was because he filled that entire tray thing they had him in. When he got home, he was just as challenging as Mandy during those first weeks. I stand corrected. He was more challenging as he couldn't make it two hours without eating again. When we took Barb and Nick to the family doctor for their three month checkup, the doctor was so much more concerned with Barb's health than he was Nick's. I know Barb had not slept more than two hours at a time for several weeks. The doctor told us to put some rice cereal in that boy's milk so he could get a full tummy. What a blessing that night was. He slept for about six hours. If felt like an eternity as we needed every minute of it. When we finally woke up, we were in a panic because we had not heard from him. He was so content. I felt we had turned a corner and soon we would be out playing catch. Silly dad, I still had a few years to go before we would do much more than what we had done for Mandy. Raising babies was a lot of work.

Then that thing that happens to women started up again. We didn't have an infant in the house anymore and Barb loved holding babies. Don't misunderstand me, she loved her children and had immense joy with them every day, but they were not babies, and the idea of another baby was on Barb's mind. This led to the most difficult time of our relationship. While I loved my children, I did not want anymore. Barb on the other hand wanted more. She didn't know how many more, but she wanted more. This struggle between us went on for many months. I tried getting Barb around the babies at the church to see if that wouldn't somehow satisfy this feeling she was having. Somehow spending more time with other people's babies just made her want one of our own. What were we to do. As a father, I was seeing all the challenges of raising another child while Barb was seeing all the blessings of raising another child. Ultimately, I won the argument but lost the blessing. I clearly was short sighted in my long-term view of life. I had deprived Barb of the family she had wanted. Let's face it, I was the number one jerk of all times.

As the years went by and the kids grew into teenagers, Barb started to think I might have been smarter about our family planning. The truth is while raising teens are challenging at times, I had some of my best days as a dad with my kids during those days. It's decisions like this that can never be undone. Had I stopped to consider the scripture and what the Bible was trying to tell me about a man's family happiness, I would have agreed with Barb. I eventually apologized for my short sightedness. It's awesome that Barb loved me anyway. That is the way it has always been with Barb and me. I do dumb things and she loves me anyway. Once you start down the path of restitution with your wife, you also have to make restitution with God. Thankfully, God was ready to bless me again. I was going to be a grandpa to six amazing grandchildren. Talk about happiness in round two of life, my quiver was finally getting full of happiness.

Somehow our grandchildren came in sets of two. Nick and Adrelly always had the first in the round followed by Jon and Mandy. It's just how it worked out. Harvey was our first grandchild. We were so eager to meet him. Neither Barb nor I had any reservations about taking on the mantle of grandparent. We had lots of concerns that our kids could actually be responsible enough to be allowed to raise our grandchildren. I mean just a couple of years earlier they were both still a bit wet behind the ears. When those babies started showing up, they grew up in a hurry. I remember driving to San Diego from our home in Cheney to stay with Nick and Adrelly until Harvey arrived. We drove a U-Haul down full of stuff they had left in our shop because their initial move back to San Diego was all about whatever that Chevy Malibu could hold. We had so many household items they could use now that they had an apartment and a son coming. Harvey was late arriving of course. When the big day happened, I watched my son come tell us Harvey was here, but they had to take him to the NICU because he was having respiratory issues. The look on his face took me back to a time when I was right where Nick was. My heart broke for his pain but knowing how God had already completed a good work with Nick in my life, I was right there to encourage him to have good hope and know the Lord God was going to be there for his new family. It wasn't long before Harvey was back in the room with his parents, and we got to say hello for the first time. I melted like butter on a hot English muffin. In that moment I was completely bonded to Harvey. There would never be any sacrifice so great that I could make for him. I would love him forever.

Three months later, I got word from Jon and Mandy they were going to the hospital. After sitting in the waiting room all night, I finally got to meet Tristen. This experience never gets old. As always, Grandma gets to go first. I finally got my turn. I remember so well this little boy whose tiny head lay in the palm of my hand and his feet just barely reached my elbow. So tiny and such a happy little guy. I knew I would love him forever. There was nothing I would not sacrifice to be sure this boy was loved and cared for all his life. I was blessed to have Tristen live close to us. I get to watch him grow up. We got to do many things together over the years. This was awesome having a grandson so close by. The only thing that could have been better was to always have all my grandsons close by. But since that could not be, we made sure to get together with Harvey as often as we could. Nick and Adrelly would come to visit regularly and these two cousins became buddies. Being a grandpa means you have special responsibilities in raising a grandson. With Tristen so close by, I had many such responsibilities. The challenges of laundry and diapers were one such responsibility I took on for my first four grandchildren. I made sure my daughters had a delivery of diapers every month just to help out. As the boys got older, the idea of getting them out of pull ups and into big boy underwear was on everyone's mind. Who better to teach this to Tristen than Grandpa. When Mandy asked, I jumped at the idea of helping out. There's a lot to teaching a boy just how to do this the right way. Give a boy a tractor tire to aim at and you are well on your way to moving out of diapers.

One of my fondest memories about Harvey and Tristen is when Nick and Adrelly drove up from San Diego for a family visit. Mandy and Jon were at our house with Tristen as we all awaited their arrival. Tristen was so proud of his newly learned skill he couldn't wait to share that learning with his cousin Harvey. Now Harvey had also been training to get out of diapers but unfortunately, he didn't have a tractor tire nearby to help him advance through this training exercise. None-the-less, Tristen was going to take care of all this with an advanced training course. As soon as Harvey got out of the car, Tristen grabbed Harvey's hand, ran across the driveway and up our front yard to where the rock walled flower garden stood. In seconds both boys had their pants down and were watering the rock wall. I have a picture of this that I have saved as one of my mementos that speaks to my success as a grandpa. Two grandson's potty trained. It was a proud moment.

Barb's health issues with Colon Cancer were difficult for everyone in the family. All of us were struggling in our own ways to cope with the struggles of a beloved wife and mother. I remember getting the news from all the kids that they were expecting child number two. It happened within days of each other. Despite the issues with chemotherapy, Barb resolved in her heart it was time to beat this thing so she could get back to being a full time grandma. It was the best news ever. Later I actually watched Barb take credit for these next two babies as she believed they came just for her. I think she might have been right. Our son had just joined the Army. He had to ship off to boot camp just before Rex was to be born. Thankfully, Adrelly was able to be close to her mom during this time to care for her. As Harvey had arrived quickly, the doctors were concerned about the delivery of Rex and urged Adrelly not to delay in getting to a hospital when labor started. They were right. It happened fast. I had the utmost compassion and appreciation for Adrelly as she had to deliver Rex in the car ride to the hospital as her mom drove frantically to get them to the delivery room. Funny thing about Rex, he was born on the freeway next to the offramp to our old church at ACF. Almost like his way of connecting with Grandpa. We were so proud of Adrelly and her beautiful son. We could hardly wait to make a trip down to visit them. We got to reconnect with all Adrelly' s wonderful family. It was an amazing time. However, I had one thing to do as the new grandpa. Reporters from the local TV stations were harassing our family wanting to know more about the story of Rex's arrival. Rex always knows how to grab a headline. I took care of that. This was a time for family. A time for a mom and a baby to be together without the world wanting to butt in. Once they knew Rex was a healthy little guy, they agreed to honor our request for family privacy so we could get to know our new grandson. Once again, after Grandma got her turn with Rex, I got to hold this little boy and bond with him. In an instant I knew he was going to be a special boy and I would love him forever and sacrifice anything to make sure his life was full and blessed. Rex has not disappointed. More than either of his brothers, Rex loves to visit the ranch and be with our horses. He connects with them in a very special way. Sometimes when he visits and life gets too chaotic, I see him go outside and run down to the corral and just love on my horses. It's like they know his spirit and are so good around him. Nick was away at boot camp when his son was born. I wanted more than anything for Nick to get to connect with Rex and Adrelly as soon as possible. I was able to order tickets so they could travel east and see Nick. I have to imagine this was an amazing time together as a new family.

Six days after Rex made his arrival, Barb and I had to depart quickly to get back to Cheney in time to meet our first granddaughter. Brooklyn was about to come into this world, and I didn't want to miss it. Grandma wasn't the only one anymore who loved to hold babies. Especially when those babies were my grandbabies. Having three grandsons, you might think this was getting routine. Nope! When I got my turn to meet Brooklyn for the first time my crusty old self turned to Jell-O. What a beautiful granddaughter I was blessed to behold. She was so tiny compared to the boys. Right then and there I knew I would love her all my life. I would sacrifice and protect her in any way necessary. Don't get me wrong, I love the rough and tumble of boys, but this little girl stole a part of my heart that I didn't know I had to give. She looked so much like her mom. As she grew up, I would look into her big hazel eyes and see a time when her mother was a child. It takes you back in a hurry. I love to see Brooklyn interact with her brother and cousins. She may be small, but she is mighty. The boys all treated her with love and respect. When Harvey met her as toddlers, he would take her by the hand and help her across the yard to make sure she didn't stumble. Brooklyn also loved the horses. Again, I am blessed to have her close by, where we can spend so much time together. While she loves baking and doing girly crafts with Grandma, she is always ready to jump into the horse corral with Grandpa and love on those horses. The first time she got up on one of our horses, she just grabbed that big old horse and loved on her. She didn't want to get down. Eventually, she laid down up there and took a nap. She has been a cowgirl ever since.

All the kids were in town, and we were blessed to spend time with all four grandchildren. Grandma loved shopping for the grandkids and I'm pretty sure their parents didn't mind the shopping excursions either. There was a small kids clothing store in town that had all the cute outfits for the kids. On one trip where we were supposed to just get something for each of the kids, I left with six oversized shopping bags full of new clothes for all the kids. It was a Tuesday. I remember so well because that was a special day at this store known as Grandma Day. Oh yeah. Grandmas got a big discount on their day. While I tried to express temperance and moderation, this was not going to happen. Grandma had a heart full of love and grandpa was going to pay for it. I finally got to the cashier who was a bit overwhelmed by the checkout experience. Seems they had to tally out the purchase four times just to get the card authorization to process. Now that's love. I wasn't very good at doing what I preached. Anytime those kids needed anything, I was all in and would do what I could. Grandma was quick to point out the lack of equality in our go to market practices. I learned my lesson and started to enjoy the experience more.

As if I couldn't be any happier, we got news that Flint was coming as grandchild number five. We were blessed for a while as the Army had stationed Nick and Adrelly much closer to us in Ft Lewis, which was just a five hour drive from our home. We took advantage of every opportunity to see them while they were here. We especially were not going to miss out on being there when Flint arrived. We headed over to Ft Lewis to help, as Harvey and Rex were in need of supervision while mom and dad were away at the hospital. We were eager to help. We had an excellent time with the boys while we awaited Flint's arrival. The day finally got here, and we got to meet Flint. Once again, Grandma got to go first and took all the loving she could give him before an impatient Grandpa demanded his turn. Such a little guy who would be so full of fun. The crazy thing, it happened again. As soon as I looked into his big brown eyes, I knew I would be forever changed. This little boy was to be my last grandson and I would love him forever and would sacrifice whatever was required for his wellbeing. Adrelly and Nick were both so happy to have their family. Again, I give great respect to Adrelly who has been able to keep her home together despite having to raise four boys who like to rough and tumble and leave Legos everywhere. That's right. I said four. I'm not sure if Nick will ever grow up. I kind of hope not. He gets right into the middle of it and while Flint may be the youngest, he holds his own. He is definitely growing up to be a city boy. After Ft Lewis, the Army sent the kids to Tokyo for about three years. That was the hardest three years as they were so far away. We got to go visit them once while they were there. And they got to come visit us once as well. Flint's first day at our home was wonderful. I think his brothers had prepared him for the visit. As soon as they got out of the car, they all took off running to the pasture to visit the horses. Harvey and Rex scaled the fence and ran about a half mile, and each grabbed a horse by the halter and walked them up to the house just like they did this every day of their life. Flint was instructed to stay close to mom, but his excitement was growing as the horses got closer. When he couldn't stand it anymore, he let out a call to the horses, Moo! It was the sincerest Moo I think I ever heard as he tried to call the horses over for a visit. Adrelly and I lost it as we couldn't stop laughing. After a long and grueling trip, I'm sure she needed a good laugh. Flint would have a special place in our family. While they live in Ft Knox Kentucky, Flint is always the first one to just into the facetime screen to get time and attention with the grandparents. We always look forward to our visits.

Last but by no means the least, we were looking forward to our last grandchild, our last granddaughter, Oakley. Mandy had a difficult pregnancy with Oakley. It was a blessing in many ways when Oakley arrived in the family. Oakley's arrival was no less complicated than the pregnancy. She was a couple weeks late arriving but managed to show up just in time for Christmas. We had a Christmas blessing. Mandy and Jon had planned all season long to have a Christmas celebration with their children. But Christmas eve was another matter as those labor pains took center stage. Mandy was determined to make sure Tristen and Brooklyn had their Christmas morning but wanted to take every precaution to be sure the kids had Barb and I there to watch them when they needed to take off to the hospital. Mandy decided to pack up everything and come to our house for the duration. We had dinner together and put the presents under the tree that night for the kids. By morning, the contractions were progressing, but Mandy wanted to be sure she was able to share Christmas morning with Tristen and Brooklyn before she headed out to the hospital with Jon. Somehow, she did it. I don't know how she did it but she did. As soon as the last gift was opened, she turned to Jon and said, let's get going right now. They left and we played with the kids all day checking in regularly for updates on Oakley's arrival. The day turned to nighttime, and we put the kids down to bed expecting a call from Jon any minute with the wonderful news. The next morning came about, and we still had no news. I tried to reach out to Jon to see how they were doing when he told me Oakley had been born just before midnight Christmas day. Barb and I were pleased to hear the news and Jon was so tired he couldn't believe he forgot to call us. I still remember Mandy's voice in the background, when she said, "you mean you didn't call mom and dad?" We eventually all let him off the hook because this beautiful little girl was such a treasure. We loaded up Tristen and Brooklyn to take them to see their little sister. They all climbed up in the bed with their mom as she introduced Oakley to them. What a precious memory that will always be in my mind. On the other hand, now there were even more people ahead of me before I got to meet my granddaughter. I patiently waited my turn. I grabbed hold onto this little girl all swaddled in a little pink blanket. I had the feeling this one was going to be trouble for me. She stole my heart in a second and I knew I would love her forever. I couldn't believe that after two children who married two more wonderful people that I called my kids and five more grandchildren that I would have room in my heart to love anyone else. But I did and it was like there was a place in my heart full of love I didn't know I had for Oakley just like there had been for all the ones before her. She is so precious and so loving. I treasure any chance I get to spend time with just her. She has so much to tell grandpa and like me, she is a big tease. There is no sacrifice I would not make to be sure she has a full and blessed life.

So here I am forty plus years later living a blessed life with a quiver full of them. I think sometimes my kids think we want the grandkids more than them. That couldn't be further from the truth. But something happens to an old man when he becomes a grandpa. He starts to see his children all over again. All the sudden he has patience eternal and a tempered perspective on the craft of raising children. True, we do get tired because these kids have so much energy. I seriously believe just sitting and watching them play can wear us out. And yes, we do get to give them back to their parents when we are tired, but as soon as they are gone, we miss them and start looking forward to our next reunion. The real truth about grandchildren is more about second chances to love your children the way you had always hoped you could. The fact that all the sudden grandpa has endless amounts of money for McDonalds when that wasn't possible when the kids were home growing up, has nothing to do with playing favorites. Children are just a joy. Just like the Bible says. Not only a joy but they also fill your hearts with love. That's why fathers and grandfathers stand at the gate to fight off those that would harm our children and try to steal away their precious hope of a happy life. My quiver is full, and the presence of God looks at me through the eyes of each one of these children. I stand diligently to help guide them through the snares and tribulations of this life. I find peace with a God who created us and loves us all so much. God knew how much I needed to know his love for his children. I experience God's love and presence each and every time I see any of my children or grandchildren. I get to hold that love and care for it and mentor it is the admonition of our Holy Father.

It just doesn't get any better than this folks. It just couldn't get any better but when I turn to my Heavenly Father, I know better is coming as he prepares to receive me someday in his house. I can just feel the warmth and excitement in my arrival someday as I explore his home and abide in his loving arms. What an amazing plan God had for families. How abundantly he provided a love for us. I also know that God looks down on my family having already loved us forever and having already made every sacrifice ever needed for our happiness. I am humbled but still strive to demonstrate this same love to the precious family God has given me.

Chapter Nineteen: Freedom to Retire

Trust in the Lord and do good; dwell in the land and enjoy safe pasture. Take delight in the Lord, and he will give you the desires of your heart. Commit your way to the Lord; trust in him and he will do this. Psalms 37:3-5

I had always hoped someday I would be able to retire early and enjoy my later years just living with Barbie and enjoying our family. I had hoped to get to this day by age 55 but it seems there were unexpected events that delayed our start just by a few years. By unexpected things, I mean things like weddings and grandchildren. I don't know why I thought these were unexpected and I certainly enjoyed these events in my life. I guess poor planning on my part. This plan to retire had a few key events which had to take place before I could kick retirement into motion. The first of which was to move out of California; cash out the equity from our home and move somewhere rural where our cash would more than cover the cost of the new home. Hopefully there would be some left to put some away for retirement as well. The other was to max out our 401K savings as well as set aside post tax savings to get us through until we reached retirement age.

I wasn't sure where I was going to move at first. I knew it could be anywhere in the western US as that was my initial coverage area for work. I considered all the smaller cities with a robust airport. An airport was important to me as I spent much of my work time traveling for business. As this was really starting to wear on me, getting to a smaller airport would be a good bridge experience until I finally retired. While I lived in Alpine California, I used the San Diego International Airport. It was a forty-minute drive to the airport. Upon arrival, I would spend about thirty minutes looking for a parking space. Then I would spend another hour getting through security check points. In all the departure plan for San Diego required me to leave about three hours before departure in order to just make the plane. When I considered at least one departure a week, this added up to a big part of my life. And while returning home was a bit quicker, it was still a good hour upon arrival before I could get to the house. I felt departing from a smaller airport would be much better. I also considered the tax implications of living in California. Escaping the state income tax and their excessive property taxes would offer more cash to stash away for retirement. This turned out to be a much larger benefit than I had considered. Fortunately realizing this early saved me from moving to Sacramento or Fresno. I was down to a few smaller cities like Boise, Spokane or maybe Reno. After our visit to Cannon Beach where we celebrated my mother-in-law's eightieth birthday, it was clear to me we needed to be closer to family and closer to the Northwest which we still called home.

We finally decided on Spokane, and we made the move in 2008. I could get from my desk to the airport gate in less than thirty minutes. I continued to get things ready for retirement. When we bought our home, we knew there would be some remodeling required to make it work perfectly for us. While the home had a large finished basement, I wanted to be sure we had upstairs space so we could avoid stairs as we got older. We did additions to the home in two projects. Finally, the home was just as we had wanted. I still had all this land and wanted to get it ready for retirement. I had acquired an old John Deere 1020 Tractor shortly after I moved onto the property. The tractor would be perfect to assist in all the work I had to do at the new ranch. Fencing was a big part of the project. I wanted to move to a small ranch so I could return to having horses like I did when I was a boy. Not that I am a big horse rider, but these ponies are my buddies. I wanted to be sure they were well cared for and kept safe on the property. I knew with grandchildren around I didn't want barbed wire or electric fencing. So over time I either contracted the work or installed fencing on my own. Barns had to be restored and painted. I needed to create better feeding areas for the horses and the goats. I decided to install a couple of heated watering stations. The hay barn had to be doubled so I could keep enough hay on hand. I think you're getting the idea now. I had a lot to do.

As all this work started to get finished, I also realized getting older meant I needed some things to be easier. While I loved that old tractor, putting snow chains on it was a huge undertaking. Those chains were well over 100 pounds each and hard to manage. I decided there would be one last investment before I took on the final chase to start retirement. I had to have a new four-wheel drive tractor that would not require chains.

Tristen and I drove down to Yakima to pick up this new tractor. He was prouder of this machine than I was. To this day he still says it's his tractor because he went to get it. That boy can and will drive anything with wheels. He and I spent lots of time around the ranch doing all kinds of things. He learns from me, and I get a smart and strong little guy who bends much better than I do. We make a great team. Tristen was seven years old when he and I did an overnight road trip to get this tractor. He was incredibly excited to go out with grandpa and to pull a big trailer to haul that tractor back home. What I didn't expect was the one thing he was most looking forward to on the trip. This little guy had decided in his own mind that once he got away from his mom and his sisters, he would be able to engage in what he called, "boy talk". I got worried about ten miles out from home when Tristen asked me if it was ok to have some boy talk since it was just us guys. I didn't quite know what to say. I didn't want to encourage bad behavior, but he was clearly anxious to share an experience with his grandpa now that it was just the two of us. His mom had always told him to be respectful of others and especially around ladies and not have potty talk unless you're outside with Grandpa or something. Not that grandpa ever encouraged such behavior, but boys will be boys. I know having four grandsons that there is nothing funnier to a boy than to laugh about certain bodily functions. I reluctantly agreed and told Tristen if this got out of hand it would have to stop because not all boy talk is considered proper even with grandpa.

The next thing I heard out of Tristen's mouth was "Diddle Poopy Diarrhea!" He could barely say these words because of the excessive laughter coming from deep within his young man's brain. I started laughing, which even delighted him more. He just kept repeating this same phrase over and over as if he was some foul-mouthed sailor or something. I guess in the mind of a seven year old, he thought he was running amuck. The laughter continued as he wanted to talk about times when he had passed gas inappropriately and so on. This went on for the entire trip to Yakima which was about four hours. We got to the hotel, I got him some snacks for the night and we turned in. He was still chucking about his day in his head and assured me I was going to experience the worst night's sleep ever as it would be noisy and unpleasant. Somehow, I survived the night. The next morning, we had the typical hotel breakfast buffet. He loved it as it had all his favorites and then we were off to pick up the tractor.

I closed the deal and paid for the tractor. As soon as the tractor was loaded on the trailer bed, Tristen had already assumed his position in the driver's seat claiming his rightful place as owner of this new tractor he bought for us. He couldn't wait to get it home so he could take it on a ride with grandpa. As we started home, I guess he realized he only had a few more hours of boy talk before he had to behave more civilized at home. And so, it started again. The boy laughed for three straight hours until we passed Ritzville when he passed out of pure exhaustion from all the laughter. I don't think I had ever heard a kid laugh so hard for so long and have so much fun. Before we got back to Cheney, I made sure Tristen had all this silliness out of his system and promised he would return to the normal decorum expected of him. I think he was ready as well. The entire experience was almost surreal as this little guy seemed to have years' worth of nonsense that needed to find its way out. What a great time we had bonding. Now I was even more determined to get this retirement started. How could I miss out on all these great experiences with my family. I needed to start making final preparations.

I started praying with Barbie about the timing and to make sure she was ready for this as well. For years, Barbie had been asking me one question over and over. "What are you going to do with yourself when you're retired?" I can translate this for any men who didn't fully understand the purpose of the question. What this really meant was more like, you better find stuff to do and not just sit around here bothering me. I was clear about one thing, while I worked from home in my downstairs office, the upstairs was Barb's domain. Our home had been her domain for almost forty years, and I knew she needed her space to maintain her own sanity. Even Barbie was ready to get me off the road and have me home much more than I had been. Despite telling me for years that she couldn't miss me unless I was gone, she really did not like being alone at home anymore. It was like something had changed in her and she also wanted to have our retirement time together. Our hearts were united on this, and it was clear to use that God had set things in motion to launch our retirement.

I sought out a local financial planner who could help discuss my situation and determine the viability of my plans. I considered various advisors but chose Thomas who was affiliated with my local credit union. After a few meetings with Thomas, he had persuaded both Barb and I, we were financially able to step away from work and begin retirement. Our affairs were in order. We had nothing left to do to get ready. But I could feel God telling me one more time, he had a special plan ready for me. I spent time in prayer as God revealed this plan to me. Basically, I was going to discuss a separation plan with my company who would then compensate us by coming to an orderly separation. I shared the plan with Thomas who thought I was nuts. There was no way this big company would ever agree to such terms. It took a bit of finesse, but everything fell into place. By finesse, I really meant being patient while God completed the work he wanted to do for me. So, at age 58, I called up my president. I told him I was done. I didn't want to work anymore but I would be reasonable with the company and facilitate a smooth transition if they would make the retention time worth my while. After a couple of weeks of discussion, they came back with a two-year transition plan. I stopped him immediately even before hearing the offer and suggested the timing was too long. I was really looking for a reason to return to work on Monday.

Fortunately for me, the business I lead was just starting to grow. Profits were better than they had ever been. I had created a five-year plan to transform the business. Many of the executives were eager to see this come about. I guess it's always a good idea to go out on a high note. After a few weeks we came to an agreement to have me stay through the end of the second quarter. During this time my replacement would be named, and I would transition my business over. Thomas was amazed how God had provided for us to launch our retirement. This all happened just as the big shut down for the 2020 Covid Pandemic hit the economy. Talk about God's timing. The business culture would forever be changed by this event, and I was fortunate to escape when I did. The pandemic also offered several opportunities for me which I had not anticipated. It took me almost another eighteen months before I fully disengaged from the industry. I was definitely retired but still had my hands in the pot. Then one day I realized it was time to completely let go. I stopped all the consulting gigs, and even signed off Indeed and all other connections I had to the industry. I have no regrets. I had been blessed with a great career and had a rich experience with the people who worked closest to me. I really didn't know what was going to replace this activity in my life, but I knew it didn't really matter. I was going to enter my golden years with a simple, slow paced deminer. Unlike many people I had known who couldn't find happiness in retirement, I was completely satisfied. When I shut off that company phone, I felt a freedom like I had not had in so many years of my life. My calendar was now completely open to me. No one could jump into my schedule and redirect my plans. I was truly free to begin this phase of my life.

Barbie was glad to have me home. I did stay busy doing various things that had been on my to-do list. I bought a park bench to place out in the corral. Sometimes I would just go out and sit with the horses and just spend time enjoying God's creation from their point of view. Barb also convinced me to get a camper which ultimately led to a new truck and a bigger camper. I said for years I could never get into camping. My idea of roughing it was staying at a Holiday Inn. Not that I was that picky, but I found this camping experience for the two of us to be great fun. Sometimes we would get away with grandkids which made the experience even better.

I had spent forty-three years in the same industry working for three companies of which I retired from the last one after twenty-seven years. I had been blessed with a steady path where God provided for our income needs. I had been fulfilled being able to lead the most excellent teams of people. I was able to create winning business strategies and steer the way forward in ways that impacted hundreds of people. I had turned a losing business into a very profitable business and even as I was leaving, I knew the people I left behind would be well cared for in the years ahead. It was important to finish strong not just because I always felt compelled to work as God had trained me to do. But in doing, I was completing all the ambitions within my own self, so nothing was left pending or unsatisfied. I hope you understand what a blessing it was to my soul to finish the way God provided. I didn't need to look back. What was ahead was somewhat unknown and I was anxious about nothing except how to live in peace with God and not to annoy Barb. It was so good to wake up from that first night's rest without having to grab a phone or run down to the office to start the day. I remember us just lounging around having coffee together and then spending time outside that day.

Psalms 37:3-5 has been a guiding passage of scripture in my life. So many people miss the meaning of this and hope to find God a dispenser of blessing upon request as if one were inserting coins in a bubble gum machine. Fortunately, God taught me the purpose of this teaching and it starts with Trusting God and following his precepts and instructions for our life. It does matter how you live in this world as a believer. Living by faith and trusting in God's faithfulness is just the beginning. God has a journey for each of us so that we can discover how deep and how great and how wide is God's love for us. I also learned in doing, I could find happiness in this life despite all the troubles and chaos the world would put before me. It was important to never accept defeat but always delight in my God who is able to complete a good work in me. I find the closer I get to God, the more I found the desires of my heart could be fulfilled. I put all my trust in God, and he did not disappoint. No pun intended but to say that I am dwelling in safe pastures is beyond my wildest desires. The last years approaching retirement, God has revealed his presence to me in everything around me. He completed the work he had for me and has set me in a place where I can be at peace with God, my church and my family.

I don't want to suggest I expect a rose garden way forward into retirement. God is not finished with me yet. I hoped to find more purpose in serving him and serving his people. I expected more difficulty as I continued to lean on my savior. The one thing I can expect is to find my God ahead of me preparing the way for me as each day unfolds. I am so thankful to be a child of God. I am so grateful for all he has done for me. I look forward to what's next knowing it will bring more delight in my relationship with Jesus. God prepared every part of me for this day. I know the trust I have for tomorrow as I rest in how God has prepared that day for me as well.

Chapter Twenty: Pray for Me Jesus

Be joyful in hope, patient in affliction, faithful in prayer. Romans 12:12

With retirement living in full swing, we soon realized what was ahead of us. Barb and I had considered plans to travel the northwest leading backyard bible clubs from our RV for small rural church congregations. I was hoping to get involved in the local food bank as Barbie was becoming more active with the ladies in our church. We were even blessed with amazing new neighbors who would become dear friends. Like us they had also come into retirement and shared a passion for this community to enjoy their golden years.

Despite the plans we were considering, God had another path for us. It was not something I had considered but it was clearly going to be something we had to face together. Since Barb's bout with Colon Cancer in 2012, she had been having this reoccurring issue with growths on her back. We didn't understand this very well but recognized they needed to be removed. Each time one was removed another would come back. Finally, a large growth had to be removed in 2017. There were many complications with this healing properly, but we endured and eventually this all worked out. So, we moved on. We were told by our oncologist to let her know if any growth returned. We continued to monitor this still not fully understanding what was really happening to Barb.

In late 2018, we started to notice a small area near the last incision area where it appeared as if something was starting to organize again. We asked our primary care doctor to look at it. He dismissed it suggesting it was nothing more than scar tissue from the former wound area. As time progressed this area seemed to get larger, and it also started to bring pain and discomfort to Barb. We tried to reach the Oncologist but were told we needed a referral from our PCP to get an appointment with her. This had nothing to do with insurance but rather a way to screen out unneeded patients away from the busy oncologists. We returned again to our primary care physician who again dismissed this as nothing but growing scar tissue. As the pain continued, he would prescribe various medications to relive the pain, but nothing was helping. I got more determined to get assistance for Barb. I once again went to see our physician demanding better care. He assured us it was scar tissue but if we wanted to get a CT scan to satisfy our curiosity, he would reluctantly agree to do so. A CT was ordered, and the doctor assured us there were no tumors in the area and we were just dealing with scar tissue. I felt somewhat relieved to know there were no tumors. Barb and I moved forward thinking we needed to find ways to deal with the scar tissue which now consumed most of the area between her shoulder blades. I think she could have made peace with the gnarly appearance except for the pain that persisted without relief. In a final cry of desperation, I called the doctor's office and asked him to allow us to see a dermatologist to evaluate options for the treatment of scar tissue. It was July 2020, about two weeks into our retirement when the visit with the dermatologist occurred. The doctor examined Barb and immediately stated this was not scar tissue. He wasn't sure what it was but was concerned. He took a biopsy and sent it off for evaluation.

It took over two months before we learned the so-called scar tissue was actually neurofibromas that had now grown to a large tumor mass. The doctor did not feel the mass was operable and encouraged us to seek support from a pain management clinic. Knowing we needed to get back to our Oncologist, I asked if he would send the referral so we could be seen by the oncologist who had treated Barb so well for so many years.

We were quickly able to get an appointment. Initially this doctor was confused as to why we would come to her with another neurofibroma. I assured her we needed her support and asked if there was nothing else to assess Barb and suggest next steps. She agreed. As soon as she looked at her back she was shocked beyond words. Then she wanted to know why we allowed this to grow without any treatment. I shared our experience with our primary physician. While she tried to avoid calling him a complete quack, she decided to get a Pet CT and further biopsies to assess Barb's condition more broadly. We soon learned Barb also had developed sarcomas in the tumor mass which had turned into MPNSP which is a very rare type of cancer. This doctor got us connected with the Fred Hutchinson Cancer Center for treatment in Seattle. She was certain Barb needed a research-based treatment team to direct her care. While she offered her support for any local treatments, she knew Barb's tumor mass needed much more support than was available in our local hospital.

I was furious with our primary care physician. Not only had he not taken the proper precautions to get Barb to better care, but I also then learned the CT he ordered of the chest was never designed to evaluate the soft tissue on her back. I reached out to the company who supervised this doctor and expressed my frustration. Despite our making every effort to get ahead of this matter, he had not given the best care we needed. In fact, he gave us a false positive test assessment from the CT. The misdiagnosis just gave this mass more time to grow.

The doctors in Seattle were amazing but knew little about neurofibromas. None the less, they researched the condition and brought us the very best available plan for treatment. They confirmed the mass was so large it was inoperable. We had one path for chemotherapy treatments but were not certain this would help. We then learned Barb's condition was very rare not only given the types of tumors but also given the size of the tumors. She was determined to align with patients of similar condition to be one out of every one-hundred-million people in the country. So basically, that meant there were only four or five other people in the entire country who had what Barb had. This meant there were no mainstream treatments available, and the team would have to choose from the best available options to determine a path of treatment. The Pet CT also found an area that lit up in the colon area where Barb had formally had the 2012 cancer removed. The doctors wanted to have this evaluated with a gastrologist.

Just when I think life is going to get simple, then I realize I must look into the face of the unknown and completely rely on God to keep going the right way. As discussions continued with the medical company, they were cautious to accept any responsibility for their doctors' actions. I assured them I did not want to take any legal actions, but I did want this doctor to be reprimanded and given oversight to insure he did not continue such careless practices. During the investigative process, I learned this physician was scheduling up to eight patients an hour which was the maximum revenue cycle he could achieve and sought to cycle patients through offering prescriptions and moving to the next billable patient. I asked the company to help us get another primary care physician and they did. Otherwise, we had an excellent team of doctors. And while no one accepted responsibility for wrongdoing, the company did agree to cover any out-of-pocket expenses required for Barb's treatment. I felt some comfort in the resolution, but I really wanted to focus on Barb and not attempt to spend time in court proceedings trying to seek justice for this doctor's misconduct. Again, God told me to move on and put my whole focus on Barb. We had unknown issues to still be evaluated. I was starting to become anxious as I did not want Barb to have to deal with one more thing.

The day came for the evaluation of her colon. I think they had to do several different tests as the area was difficult to reach with their instruments. I actually think this was the second test and I sat along with my mask on during the middle of a pandemic awaiting news from the doctors as to the question of possible colon cancer having returned after many years. I once again sought the prayers of family and friends. I could not find the kind of comfort with God that I had come to expect. All this uncertainty was shaking me but not my foundation. I was determined to rely upon God even though Barb and I had crossed the lines of health care into the abyss of the unknown care for rare diseases. I sat there just outside the door to the treatment area waiting for Barb to return to the recovery area. I was praying in ways I couldn't even begin to know how to pray. My heart would just simply burst open with all this emotion, and I couldn't even get words to describe to God what was truly on my heart. I just didn't want one more thing. I was trying to pray for a negative screening, but I just couldn't pull myself together with the boldness and the courage to ask my Heavenly Father for this one more thing.

Then it hit me. I had a friend in Jesus who could come and teach me how to pray. In fact, Jesus often offered to pray for others in efforts to teach us to pray. I stopped all the spinning in my heart and soul and asked Jesus to pray to our Heavenly Father for Barbie. To my amazement, which is another matter of my spiritual maturity to deal with, I heard Jesus begin to pray. Here is what I heard, "Father, I come to you to pray for all the people in this clinic who are anxious and desperately seeking your healing. I love these people and Father I know you also love them with all your heart. Father if it be pleasing to you, please do not let one person in this clinic leave here today facing a diagnosis of cancer, and especially for Barbie whom you love so dearly."

What could I say? I was so blessed to have my dearest friend in Jesus speak to the Father on my behalf and to teach me how to pray. I was so overcome with the truth of this prayer I turned to God in thanksgiving and repentance for making this all about me when so many are loved by God and hurting. I was assured by Jesus that he would be with us through this time of sufferings as he loved both of us so much. We finally got the determination from the doctor that the reading of the CT was not perfect, and he could find nothing that needed further treatment. Jesus' prayer had been heard and answered that day. I am pretty sure everyone in that clinic also got healing news because Jesus prayed for them offering intersensory prayer to the Father in Heaven just as he said he would do for us.

Once again, I had experienced the presence of God in my life in a way that looked beyond the unknown and searched my heart for a place to anchor in truth. After being a faithful disciple for over fifty years walking with Jesus, I had never asked him to pray for me. It seems such a simple thing to do and the Bible clearly tells us this is one of the things Jesus is doing for us now that he is on the right-hand throne by the Father. I have so much more to learn about living and walking with God. I am certain my experiences with God will continue to amaze me. I am certain he will also be there by my side. I want to share one more story about my Great Grandfather White as I close this book. As my mom went thru her grandfather's old bibles, she came across this handwritten sermon notes stuffed in the pages of his old preaching bible. She was amazed while reading his sermon notes, as she had heard the words before but not from her grandfather who had spent much of his time as an Assembly of God Minister. My mom asked her grandfather where he found this poem. He responded by saying it was a little something he wrote. In his later years he never realized this poem which to that time had an anonymous author was so popular in Christian culture. When my mom shared this story with me, I realized that my Great Grandfather might have written a poem not only for his sermon that Sunday morning but something that would also inspire me in my walk through the challenges of this life. To know my great grandfather had experienced sufferings and leaned on Jesus over a hundred years before, brought assurance God's promises were enduring. I will share this with you now as you can see how God sent this blessing down through our family to help me face the great ordeal of life while being in the presence of God who loves us.

Footprints in the Sand

A pilgrim arrived in heaven and God said to him, "Would you like to see where you've come from?"

When the pilgrim responded that he would, God unfolded the story of his whole life and he saw footprints from the cradle to the grave.

Only there were not only the footprints of the pilgrim, but another set of prints alongside.

The pilgrim said, "I see my footprints, but whose are those?"

And the Lord said, "Those are My footprints. I was with you all the time."

Then they came to a dark, discouraging valley and the pilgrim said, "I see only one set of footprints through that valley.

I was so discouraged. You were not there with me. It was just as I thought—I was so all alone!"

Then the Lord said, "Oh, but I was there. I was with you the whole time.

You see, those are MY footprints. I carried you all through that valley."

About the Author

Born in Paris Tennessee, I lived out in the country as my father managed the local print shop for the newspaper and my mom worked at the factory just beyond my granny's house. It was a simple life until I turned the age of eight and my father left it all to join the ministry as a pastor. We moved about two hours away so he could attend college to prepare him for the work of a pastor. His ministry kept us moving around West Tennessee until we moved to Covington Washington in 1978 as I was seventeen years old. I had a brother, Ross Edward, who was about five years younger than I was and we lived with mom and dad until a sister showed up unexpectedly when I turned fourteen. She was full of energy and enjoyed all the beautiful things a daughter could expect unlike the hand-me-downs from the early years with just us boys.

I married Barbie in 1982 at the age of twenty-one. Just over two years later we welcomed our daughter Mandy and another two years we welcomed our son Nick. Our family was a tight knit clan until the kids grew up and started their own lives. Mandy married first to Jon. Two months later Nick married Adrelly. We were having a great time with the extended family. Then just a couple of years later Nick and Adrelly welcomed their first child, Harvey. Three months later Mandy and Jon welcomed their first child, Tristen. If a grandpa could be any prouder, I don't know how it could be possible and I was so thankful for my boys until I got a call from Nick and Adrelly saying Rex was on his way. About the same time Jon and Mandy told us about our first granddaughter, Brooklyn. These two were born just six days apart. I was so happy and loved my growing family and was pretty sure that was it. Then we got another call from Nick and Adrelly to tell us about Flint. A couple of months later it was Jon and Mandy's turn to tell us about our next granddaughter, Oakley. These two were only five months apart. I don't know if you see a pattern, but it seems my kids did many of the same big life experiences surprisingly together. Not coordinated or planned so we could get through one before the next, but it came in sets every time. I'm not complaining. Rather I'm telling you this, because it was awesome to grow the family two at a time. So much fun.

I spent forty-three years working in banking and financial technology services. I was able to retire early at the age of fifty-nine and continue to enjoy my retirement with Barbie.

Barbie and I have had the pleasure of serving in several churches but frequently got associated with church startups in Covington with my parents, in Alpine, to even a start up in Cheney. We now attend Cheney Community Church where we have finally found the community of believers, we have been searching for most of our life. We are home now and have agreed to finish our lives right here. In fact, if we leave this world before Jesus returns for us, we want to be fired off in fireworks over our pasture to share in the dust of the pasture we enjoyed viewing the later years of our lives.

Not sure if there is another book coming but I am thinking about it. This book was more challenging than I could have anticipated. If another book comes, it will come as God enriches my heart to share again.